Think It, Show It

Social Studies

Strategies for Communicating Understanding

Author
Gregory A. Denman, M.A.T.

Foreword by
Dylan Barth

 **Lesley**
UNIVERSITY

 SHELL EDUCATION

Publishing Credits

Corinne Burton, M.A.Ed., *President;* Conni Medina, M.A.Ed., *Managing Editor;* Emily Smith, M.A.Ed., *Content Director;* Lee Aucoin, *Senior Graphic Designer;* Marc Pioch, M.A.Ed., *Editor;* Noelle Cristea, M.A.Ed., *Editor;* Stephanie Bernard, *Assistant Editor;* John Leach, *Assistant Editor*

Image Credits

p. 75 National Archives and Records Administration [523148]; p. 79 (top) Bettmann/Getty Images, (bottom) Library of Congress [LC-USZ62-29821]; all other images from iStock and/or Shutterstock.

Standards

© 2007 Board of Regents of the University of Wisconsin System. World-Class Instructional Design and Assessment (WIDA) © Copyright 2010. National Governors Association Center for Best Practices and Council of Chief State School Officers. All rights reserved.

© Copyright 2007–2015. Texas Education Association (TEA). All rights reserved.

Shell Education

A division of Teacher Created Materials
5301 Oceanus Drive
Huntington Beach, CA 92649-1030

http://www.tcmpub.com/shell-education

ISBN 978-1-4258-1652-0

©2017 Shell Education Publishing, Inc.

Table of Contents

Acknowledgments

With love to Vickie—wife, friend, and constant companion. Her readings, corrections, and suggestions were invaluable to this book. Many times, when she got home from a full day of teaching, she would find another section for her to look over. With nothing but a smile, she would carefully read it with a red pencil in her hand.

Special thanks to Neal McCarthy, my research assistant. His extensive knowledge kept me in line with current teaching trends in social studies. I so appreciated our after-school meetings.

Next, Noelle Cristea, my editor at Teacher Created Materials. She worked with me on every page of this book. Not only did she have critical suggestions, but she patiently corrected my grammar. Throughout the process, I felt like I was working with a close friend. Also, thanks to my production editor, Marc Pioch. He took a plain manuscript and artfully fashioned it into a beautifully designed book.

Foreword

The return to writing across the curriculum has brought writing to the forefront of all subjects. While it has always been essential for historical writing to be evidence-based, the National Council for Social Studies (C3) Framework has made that emphasis even greater. Indeed, success in all content areas demands that students develop essential writing and analysis skills. The framework goes further stating that "students [must] employ complex vocabulary, understand discipline-specific patterns of language, and exercise analytical thinking skills" (3) in order to be successful.

Think It, Show It Social Studies: Strategies for Communicating Understanding has practical beginnings for both the writer and the teacher. It emphasizes modeling with clear steps for students and innovative tactics for teachers. Gregory Denman is keenly aware of the amount of content social science teachers are expected to cover while also teaching important skills like writing. The streamlined approach to the writing process he takes makes it possible for any teacher to integrate this essential skill into his or her current instruction.

Think It, Show It Social Studies: Strategies for Communicating Understanding includes a variety of types of historical writing, sample essays, graphic organizers for students, creative ideas for introducing academic vocabulary, and appendices chock-full of mentor texts for teachers and students. As Denman states, and I can attest, good writing is of course a great skill to have, but the process of becoming a good writer is a powerful learning tool. It is through the process that students become skilled thinkers, talkers, and analysts. And through the writing process, they practice effective ways of communicating their new understanding. Write on!

—Dylan D. E. Barth, Teacher
Geography and World History AP
North High School
Torrance, CA

Writing as a Learning Tool

Good writing requires good thinking, better writing prompts, and better thinking. In his book *On Writing: A Memoir of the Craft,* the novelist Stephen King states that "writing is refined thinking" (125). Indeed, it is clear that there is an important symbiotic relationship in our classroom between writing and thinking. Each supports, while prompting, the other. Across the curriculum, when students engage in content-area writing, they must think deeper about the content. This process goes well beyond punctuation and correct grammar usage. The depth of their explanations mirrors the depth of their understanding. In math, for example, students must justify the process and their mathematical thinking behind the solutions they present. In the world of scientific inquiry, they need to record the analytical procedures they use and explain and support the results they find. Social studies is no exception. Writing in social studies necessitates that students think, and think critically, to: explain, describe, analyze, construct theses, provide evidence from documents, communicate conclusions, or support arguments or claims. Writing allows students to synthesize and articulate their understanding of the concepts and content they are studying. As it has been referred to: Writing Is Thinking Made Visible.

Think It, Show It Social Studies: Strategies for Communicating Understanding was written as a result of the occurrence of two things—one nationally and one personally. The first is the 2013 publication by the National Council for Social Studies of *College, Career, and Civic Life (C3) Framework for Social Studies State Standards.* The second, as a teacher and writing consultant, is my being asked by schools and districts to specifically help social studies teachers with writing instruction.

The first influence was the publication of the C3 Framework. Its subtitle is *Guidance for Enhancing the Rigor of K–12 Civics, Economics, Geography, and History.* The framework is meant "to provide states with voluntary guidance for upgrading existing social studies standards" (NCSS 2013, 6). As stated in its introduction, "The framework aims to support states in creating standards that prepare young people for effective and successful participation in college, careers, and civic life" (NCSS 2013, 6). An element of the framework's rationale is the preparation of students for civic life, which includes that they "read, write, and think deeply" (NCSS 2013, 82). "Young people," it's stated, "need strong tools for, and methods of, clear and disciplined thinking in order to traverse successfully the worlds of college, career, and civic life" (NCSS 2013, 6).

Rooted in the C3 Framework is the critical importance of students' acquisition of college and career readiness literacy skills. "Literacy instruction," it stresses, is a "shared responsibility" between all the content areas within K–12 education (NCSS 2013, 7). In this effort, the C3 Framework was aligned with college and career readiness standards. These focus, in general, on writing process skills, such as the text types of argument/opinion, informative/explanatory, and narrative, as well as the production of "clear and coherent writing" that is "appropriate to task, purpose, and audience" (NCSS 2013, 63).

Although I refer to individual writing standards throughout this book, readers can see their entire delineation in the C3 Framework document available through the National Council for Social Studies. The bottom line, however, is this: twenty-first century teachers of social studies need to integrate rigorous, content-specific writing instruction into their classrooms.

This brings me to my work as an educator and writing consultant. Schools and districts across the country are amending their curricula to address these more rigorous academic demands. In fact, many school districts have initiated writing prompts in social studies at key grade levels as a part of their ongoing student assessment. In Denver Public Schools, for example, seventh graders are now given a writing task as an element of their Midyear Interim Assessment. On one of these assessments, students are to create graphic organizers in preparation for an essay addressing a given prompt. As a document-based question (DBQ), students are given both a primary and a secondary source document to read. In their responses to the prompt, they are to defend their points of view and address counter arguments, supported by text evidence from the documents. For students to be successful with challenging writing tasks such as this, teachers of social studies need to employ instructional techniques and strategies traditionally used exclusively in the language arts classroom. We can't simply assign and grade. We need to teach the appropriate writing skills and provide the necessary support. Therein lies a learning curve for many curriculum leaders and teachers.

Whereas elementary and intermediate teachers have probably had some or perhaps even extensive training with the writing process and writing instruction, middle school social studies teachers might not have had any training. Also, there are the very specific college and career readiness text types stressed in the C3 Framework. Even teachers trained in the writing process have needed to realign the focus of their instruction to teach to these new standards. As a result of this, I have had the opportunity to work with many social studies teachers at all grade levels to help them explore effective instructional strategies to use in their classrooms. In some instances, I have returned to districts where I had previously worked with the language arts teachers. The districts wanted not only to strengthen the writing instruction of the social studies teachers but also to build an instructional common ground among the different content areas. They wanted students to be taught with a consistent approach and with the same emphasis and focus across the curriculum—not one approach in third grade, another in fifth, and something completely different in eighth.

I certainly applauded the direction in which the schools were moving and looked forward to working with their teachers. However, when I began my presentations, I had to first address the unspoken "elephant in the room." As I introduced myself and what I was there to present, teachers rarely voiced any of their concerns to me. I believe they were being polite to me as a guest, but I knew what many of them were thinking for I'd felt similar things.

These thoughts might have been going through their minds:

- *With all the content I have to cover, how will I have time to teach writing?*

- *I teach writing in my language arts class. Isn't that enough? I have four other content areas to teach.*

- *We use a specific step-by-step writing program. Will I need to create an additional curriculum to address writing in social studies?*

- *I was trained in social studies, not English.*

- *By the way, what do sentence fragments have to do with the early causes of the Civil War?*

These, of course, are very legitimate concerns. In social studies classes, I explained, we are not teaching writing as such, but rather using writing as a learning tool. Although we employ many of the same strategies as in our language arts classes and are supporting the shared responsibility of literacy instruction, we are principally using writing as a means—a means to prompt students to think deeper about the content and to communicate a more comprehensive understanding of it. Communicating one's understanding parallels one's learning. Therefore, the time we devote to writing and writing instruction in our classrooms is time we are actually teaching social studies.

As a learning tool, writing in social studies classrooms is a process in which students are active participants in their own learning. Students are thinking, talking, and writing critically about the events and issues that they are studying. They are compiling relevant information from class notes, readings, digital and media presentations, and outside research and presenting it in a variety of formats. They are arguing or defending opinions or claims and supporting their arguments with text evidence from multiple sources. Using different mediums—both print and visual—they are explaining and elaborating on ideas or concepts from their units of study. They are digging deeper into historical events by mapping out their causes and effects. They are discovering similarities and differences between historical figures, events, and concepts. They are exploring and writing creative narratives to enrich their understanding of people and times. They are communicating their understanding.

In *Think It, Show It Social Studies: Strategies for Communicating Understanding,* I have included many of the strategies and materials I have personally used with hundreds of students—students just like yours—who are being prepared for effective and successful participation in college, careers, and civic life. When I've worked specifically with social studies teachers, I've challenged myself by asking the following question:

> What can I create that simplifies the writing process so that teachers can easily and effectively integrate it into their classes?

All teachers must teach writing—regardless of their backgrounds, past experiences or training with writing instruction—and without sacrificing precious instructional time in social studies. It is the goal of this book to respond to the following needs:

Goals of This Book

- Provide materials that teachers need which have been tailored and are best suited for use in social studies.

- Explain instructional models that can be relied on with whatever topics are part of the existing curriculum.

- Provide mentor texts, student sheets, activities, rubrics, and student exemplars that teachers can immediately use in their social studies classrooms.

Writing Process: An Overview

Social studies curriculum presents endless and creative avenues for students to write. In social studies classes, students might create any of the following products:

- arguments
- biographies
- cartoons
- descriptions
- dialogues
- diaries
- editorials
- essays
- eulogies
- historical fiction

- inscriptions
- interviews
- journals
- letters
- monologues
- news stories
- opinion papers
- parodies
- plays
- poetry

- public notices
- reaction papers
- reports
- résumés
- reviews
- skits
- slogans
- speeches
- time capsule lists
- TV shows

Success with any of these involves—to varying degrees—having students follow the stages or steps of the writing process. These stages are what writers think and do as they write and can be replicated in a classroom setting. Here is an exercise to do with students when working with the writing process.

Model It!

First, have students think of all the words they know or can think of when they hear the phrase "writing process." Record their responses on the board. Students' brainstorm may include the following words:

> brainstorming, capitalization, corrections, cue words, edit, first draft, final copy, grades, grammar, graphic organizers, partner proof, peer edit, outlines, prompts, proofread, publishing, punctuation, read, rereading, revise, rubric, scoring rubric, share, spelling, webs, word mines, Venn diagrams

Then say, "If we think of the writing process as a story with a beginning, a middle, and an end, where would each of the words that you brainstormed fall? Work with a partner to categorize our list into a three-column chart." (See the chart on page 12 for an example sort.)

BEGINNING	MIDDLE	END
brainstorming	cue words	capitalization and punctuation
graphic organizers	first draft	corrections
outlines	partner proof	edit
prompts	peer edit	final copy
Venn diagrams	scoring rubric	grades
webs		grammar
word mines		proofread
		publishing
		read
		rereading
		revise
		scoring rubric
		share
		spelling

With these lists, discuss writing as a process with beginning, middle, and end activities and with steps that can be followed as students work their way toward final written products.

This process is stressed in today's college and career readiness standards. The process includes prewriting, revising, editing, and rewriting. In classroom instruction, the writing process is commonly broken into these stages:

1. prewriting/planning
2. first draft
3. revision
4. editing
5. final draft/proofreading
6. sharing and/or publishing

It is important to know that although the writing process appears to proceed in a linear, step-by-step sequence, it really doesn't. The process has a more fluid, cyclical nature, and students sometimes need to swing back and forth between the stages. Ross M. Burkhardt (2002) includes this concept as one of his 10 fundamental assertions about writing. In his eighth assertion, he states, "Writing is a recursive process" (17). A student may discover that while working on a first draft, he or she needs an explanation of something and must revert back to the prewriting stage with research. In the same way, while revising, a student might discover that the writing's organization is illogical or doesn't read well, and he or she needs to redraft sections of text. "This recursive process continues," Burkhardt states, "until the author is satisfied that the piece is done" (20).

Prewriting/Planning

In the prewriting/planning stage, students select topics, identify the purpose and genre of writing, assemble and organize content, and generate vocabulary. To introduce students to the prewriting/planning stage, choose from the following activities:

- brainstorms
- data charts
- freewrites
- graphic organizers
- lists
- maps

- outlines
- T-charts
- Venn diagrams
- webs
- word clusters
- word mines

An example of a prewriting activity sheet to use with students is *Thinking Through Your Writing* (Figure 1.1 on page 14; reproducible on page 144). It supports students as they plan to write about specific topics. With it, students first identify topics, purposes for writing, and types of writing (e.g., argument, first-person narrative, informative/explanatory). The "Questions My Writing Will Answer" section allows students to begin to think through questions that need to be researched for the assignment, often with both primary and secondary sources. These questions function as starting points for students' research and often can be generated together as a class. Finally, students record the form in which their writing should be submitted (e.g., report, poem, newspaper article).

Figure 1.1 Thinking Through Your Writing

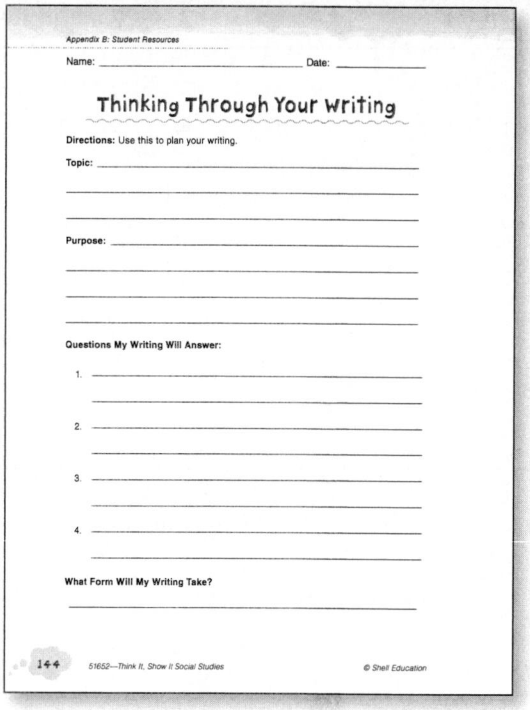
Appendix B: Student Resources

Name: ______________________ Date: __________

Thinking Through Your Writing

Directions: Use this to plan your writing.

Topic: ______________________

Purpose: ______________________

Questions My Writing Will Answer:

1. ______________________
2. ______________________
3. ______________________
4. ______________________

What Form Will My Writing Take?

____

144 51652—Think It, Show It Social Studies © Shell Education

Thinking Through Your Writing can be applied to a variety of topics and writing purposes. It can also be used with various grade levels for both beginning and advanced students. The following is an example of the first few steps with *Thinking Through Your Writing* that uses the topic of an American president.

Model It!

In preparing to write a report on an American president, a student starts with the topic "the president." The purpose and type of writing will be to give information about the life and importance of the president in an explanatory text. Next, the student begins to formulate the questions that will need to be answered and included as part of the report:

- When was he born?
- He was part of what historical era?
- What role or contribution did he play in __________ (unit of study)?
- What details do we know about his position in history?

Finally, on the sheet, the student identifies that the form or format of the final piece will be a report. While students are researching answers to their questions, have them keep running lists of the key or domain-specific vocabulary for their topics. These are the words germane to the content or domains they are exploring (e.g., *president, ratification, U.S. Constitution, served in, delegate to, framing of, Continental Congress*). The use and understanding of these words act as functioning knowledge in their writing about topics of study. With their topics, purposes for, types of writing, established content gathered, vocabulary collected, and final forms identified, students are prepared to write.

Another prewriting sheet along the same lines is the *Add a Biographical Fact Planning Sheet* (Figure 1.2; reproducible on page 145). Again, this prewriting activity has students identify their topics and write questions at the same time they are searching for interesting facts. On this sheet, they write their questions as well as the information they find during their research. Have students include citations for each of the items, indicating their text evidence. Also, to help them with the initial organization of their texts, have them write numbers next to each of their bulleted pieces of information in a probable sequence.

Figure 1.2 Add a Biographical Fact Planning Sheet

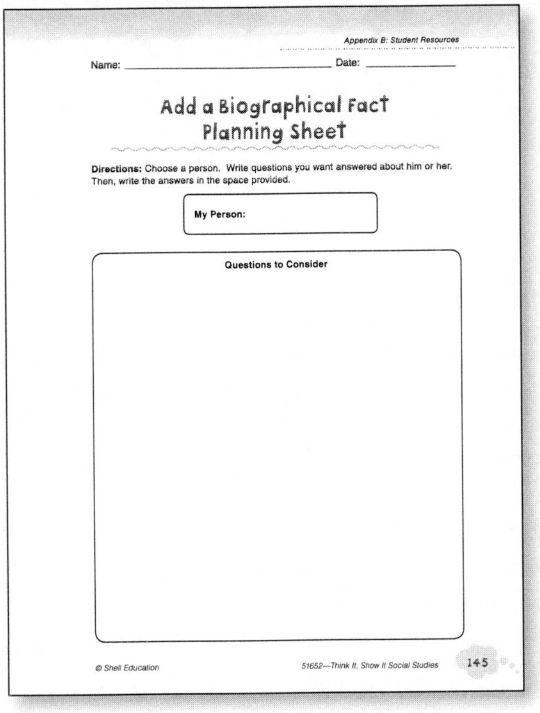

Appendix B: Student Resources

Name: _____ Date: _____

Add a Biographical Fact Planning Sheet

Directions: Choose a person. Write questions you want answered about him or her. Then, write the answers in the space provided.

My Person:

Questions to Consider

© Shell Education   51652—Think It, Show It Social Studies   145

Using the filled-in sheet, they can then write biographical fact poems. In this format, the student adds one biographical fact to each successive, repeating line. The poems are then presented as a guessing game to the class. Using the example of research with presidents, here is a sample:

Which President Am I?

A

A president

A president born in 1751

A president born in 1751, involved in the American Revolution

A president born in 1751, involved in the American Revolution, who did not sign the Declaration of Independence

A president born in 1751, involved in the American Revolution, who did not sign the Declaration of Independence, but did influence the planning and ratification of the U.S. Constitution

A president born in 1751, involved in the American Revolution, who did not sign the Declaration of Independence, but did influence the planning and ratification of the U.S. Constitution, and who declared war on Britain in 1812.

(Who am I?—*James Madison*)

Copies of both *Thinking Through Your Writing* and *Add a Biographical Fact Planning Sheet* can be found in the appendix (pages 144–145). An extension on how to use both sheets is included in chapter 6.

First Draft

Having students write first drafts is the second stage in the writing process. To write first drafts, students should use text elements and materials from the prewriting stage.

Knowing the purpose for and the intended type of writing, and having assembled the initial content and generated key vocabulary, students start writing their first drafts. During the writing, students should be busy completing many tasks: looking up synonyms, double-checking facts, going back to their sources and gathering additional information, rereading passages, and perhaps discussing ideas with someone. On their papers, they may have erasures and crossed-out words. They may have lines drawn out to their margins with extensions to sentences and ideas written out. The first draft is best described as a work in progress. At this stage, students are encouraged to write their ideas clearly and in organized ways, all the while knowing that there will be later opportunities to fine-tune their work. Although spelling, punctuation, and grammar are always important, they will specifically be addressed later in the writing process and should not be stumbling blocks at this stage.

Revision

The revision stage is where students look at the writing again, re-examine, and make changes that improve the content, organization, and clarity of their writing.

The revision process allows students to review the content of their drafts and consider what might need to be clarified, added, shifted around, or deleted. A common acronym called **ARMS** can be used to help students remember the revision process:

1. **A**dd content
2. **R**emove content
3. **M**ove content
4. **S**ubstitute for different word, idea, or example

Students should know that at the revision stage, they are reconsidering or "reseeing" their first drafts in an effort to improve them. Have them start by thinking about the questions on *Revising My Writing* (Figure 1.3; reproducible on page 147).

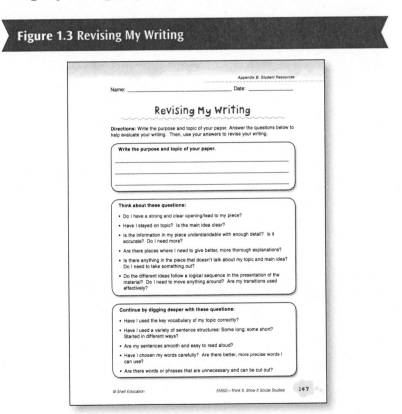

Figure 1.3 Revising My Writing

At times, it is beneficial to have students work in pairs or groups to comment on and receive feedback on each other's drafts using the same type of questioning. At this point, they are working together not only to consider the organization of the piece but also to take critical looks at the actual content. Other stylistic considerations include: *Does it engage the reader? Are sentences and vocabulary used correctly and effectively?* These are referred to as the Three Cs of Effective Writing: **C**lear, **C**oherent, and **C**orrect. Many times during the revision stage, it is best to discuss students' papers with them in short, individual writing conferences using questions, such as the following:

Writing conference Questions

- What do you think of your work so far? Are there any problems?

- Is there anything else you think you might need to say about your topic? Do you think you need more information?

- Are there places that need more details? More explanation?

- Is there another way to look at this idea or another way to explain it?

- What did you mean to say here? Can it be made clearer for the reader?

- How is this idea connected to the other ideas in the piece?

- Here you are almost repeating word for word what you said earlier. How might you revise that?

- Are there any facts that you think you might need to double-check?

Editing

The editing stage is where students identify and correct mistakes in grammar, punctuation, spelling, and capitalization. It is a time for students to specifically assess their work to look for possible mistakes with the mechanics. The acronym **CUPS** can be used to remind students what they should be looking for.

1. **C**apitalization—includes the first word of each sentence and all proper nouns

2. **U**sage—includes subject/verb agreement, homophones, sentence fragments and run-ons, and forming plurals

3. **P**unctuation—includes marks at the ends of sentences, commas in a series, commas in dates, and apostrophes in contractions and for possession

4. **S**pelling—check all questionable spelling

At this stage of the writing process, students know that they are to mark up their drafts using editing marks to indicate where they need to make corrections. It is best to use the same editing marks that are used in language arts classes. During this process, students are specifically looking for mistakes with mechanics of their writing. During the editing process, display or hand out copies of *The Editing Process* (Figure 1.4; reproducible on page 190) to help focus students' attention as they edit their writing.

Figure 1.4 The Editing Process

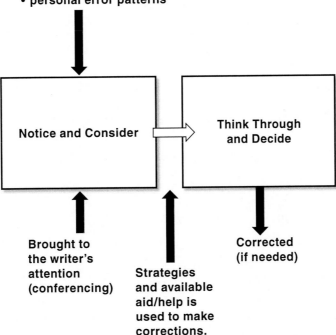

High-Glare Errors

• typical writers' problems
• personal error patterns

Notice and Consider

Think Through and Decide

Brought to the writer's attention (conferencing)

Strategies and available aid/help is used to make corrections.

Corrected (if needed)

Model It!

Students are to read their drafts, noticing and considering possible errors. Along with the many other writing issues, always focus first on the common—and maddening—homophone errors that students (and adults alike) notoriously make. These are types of high-glare errors because they are the errors we find most glaring on pages. The following is a small sampling of high-glare errors.

- its versus it's
- whose versus who's
- your versus you're

- to, two, and too
- their, there, and they're
- our versus are

Share *100 Critical Spelling Words* and *Troublesome Homophones* (pages 148–149). It is best to share these lists with students as they are editing their writing.

Besides the common writing errors, individual students have errors that are more frequently made. I call them "personal error patterns." To address these, have students maintain records of their error patterns in Writer's Notebooks. Writer's Notebooks are simple spiral notebooks that students keep for any and all writing that they complete.

The notebooks become personal, ongoing reference books for students. In the notebooks, students record the types of errors that they have frequent problems with along with strategies for how to correct them. For example, if a student has a tendency to write with sentence fragments, his or her Writer's Notebook would have strategies for recognizing and correcting fragments.

Writer's Notebook: Fixing Sentence Fragments

Strategy 1: Create two sentences by using a period and a capital.

Strategy 2: Use a comma and then a coordinating conjunction (*for, and, nor, but, or, yet, so*) to join the two thoughts. The acronym FANBOYS may help to remember these.

It is important to know that Writer's Notebooks are not static books with the same, copied pages year after year. Rather, they are ongoing reference books that evolve as students make their way through the writing process. In your classroom, if you see that students are making errors with forming plurals, have short, whole-class mini lessons on forming plurals. Students should take notes during these lessons and copy written summaries and strategies into their notebooks. Then, have them refer to their notebooks to make corrections on their papers. The same thing is true of the individual errors on papers. For example, mark misspelled critical spelling words, and have individual students reference a spelling list copied into their notebooks to correct them. The Writer's Notebook will be a critical and helpful aid during the editing process.

Furthermore, while students are going through their drafts, they are to think through and decide: *Do I need an apostrophe here? Is that the correct use of "sense"?* They then, of course, have to determine what to correct. It is also important, in the same way as the language arts class, for the social studies class to contain many reference books and aids for students to use and refer to during this process. Having marked their papers using editing marks, students are now ready to rewrite or type their final copies.

Final Draft and Proofreading

The final draft and proofreading stage allows students to find and correct errors and oversights as the final copy is completed. Students write or type their final copies, amending the text with the finalized revisions.

However, before they turn the paper in, they are to proofread it a final time. Again, they are to double-check their mechanics and conventions but also look for any oversights that might have occurred during rewriting. *Was something inadvertently left out that was meant to be included in the piece? Does something still need to be corrected? Is there anything that needs to be corrected now?* At this point, students could work together in an activity called *Partner Proofing* (Figure 1.5; reproducible on page 150).

Model It!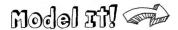

Pair up students, and assign each of them a role and responsibility: writer or reader. The writer gives his or her paper to the reader. The reader reads the paper with these responsibilities:

- Note words, sentences, or ideas that give them—as readers—difficulty.

- Note any problems with clarity—does it make sense?

- Note any mechanical errors or problems.

- Note parts that are particularly well written.

After reading, the writer and reader work and discuss the piece together. The reader points out the well-written sections and shares any writing problems he or she noted. Any editing decisions should be made together. Afterwards, they exchange roles and work with the other text.

Figure 1.5 Partner Proofing

Appendix B: Student Resources

Name: _____   Date: _____

Partner Proofing

Directions: Pair up with another student. One of you assumes the role of "the reader." The other has the role of "the writer." The writer gives his/her paper to the reader and follows his/her responsibilities. The writer follows his/her responsibilities. Afterwards, change roles.

Reader's Responsibility

Reader: _____

While Reading

- notes words, sentences or ideas that give them—as readers—difficulty

- notes any problems with clarity—does it make sense?

- notes any mechanical errors or problems

- notes parts that are particularly well written

After Reading

- points out well-written sections

- explains and discusses any writing problems with the piece

- makes editing decisions with the writer

Writer's Responsibility

Writer: _____

After Reading

- listens to the reader's responses and concerns

- makes editing decisions with the reader

150   *51652—Think It, Show It Social Studies*   *© Shell Education*

Sharing and/or Publishing

The last stage in the writing process provides students with the opportunity to acknowledge and celebrate their writing. At this stage, there are many ways to support students' writing efforts.

Ways to Share Student Writing

- Reports can be read aloud to the class and to other classes.

- Book reviews can be compiled into a class collection.

- Plays and skits can be acted out.

- Interviews can be done in costume and recorded.

- Arguments can be presented in debates.

- Speeches can be given.

- Mock newspapers that include news articles, cartoons, editorials, book reviews, and letters to the editor can be published.

- Dialogues between historical figures can be recorded and put on a class web page.

- Biographies can be visually and digitally presented.

The stages and activities of the writing process present a foundation for social studies teachers to integrate writing into their classrooms. The process was never meant to be a step-by-step procedure that has to be adhered to each and every time students do a writing assignment but rather a guideline to the structure of authentic writing instruction in social studies curriculum. Please consider the purpose and format of assignments. With informal pieces and quick writes, for example, the prewriting and editing stages may justifiably be scaled back, whereas more formal assignments warrant more thorough use of the writing process. Incorporate the different prewriting, revision, and editing strategies into instruction as they best serve the growth of students. Effective teachers, be they social studies or language arts teachers, employ the best strategies that produce the best results from their students. Chapter 2 will present an instructional model that streamlines the writing process as it can be used in your social studies classroom.

AGO: An Instructional Writing Model for the Social Studies Classroom

Figure 2.1 AGO

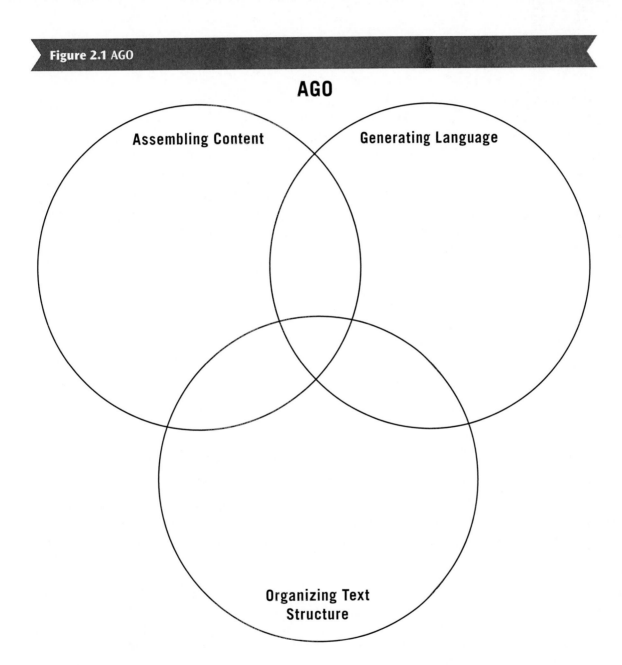

AGO

Assembling Content

Generating Language

Organizing Text Structure

Three letters can identify the three essential overlapping elements of the instructional model for your writing lessons: **A**, **G**, and **O**. The "A" represents *assembling content*. The "G" represents *generating language*. The "O" represents *organizing text structure*.

Assembling Content

Content is the basis of students' writing in social studies. They may write expository reports, compose poems based on historical figures, or create stories where geographical events are personified. The content in these pieces may be acquired from students' own background knowledge, notes taken in class, readings, research, and/or the investigation of questions. Regardless, the writing is derived from the content of social studies.

Generating Language

Embedded within the content of social studies is its key, or domain-specific, vocabulary. Students need the vocabulary to understand the content, and vice versa, the content to give them a context for understanding the vocabulary. Underpinning the historical implications and causes of the War of 1812, students need vocabulary, such as *economic sanctions*, *impressment*, and *retaliatory embargo*. Inversely, to truly understand this vocabulary beyond a memorized dictionary definition, they need the historical context in which to anchor the word. In writing (and speaking) about the content, students need to know not only the domain-specific vocabulary but also the words and patterns of sentences conventionally used for the type of writing they are doing. To demonstrate this point, match the words below with the type of writing where they are most commonly used.

As a result of; Consequently	Compare and contrast
Both; In contrast to	Persuasive
It is argued; However	Cause and effect

You should have connected "as a result of" and "consequently" to cause and effect. "Both" and "In contrast to" would be used in writing to compare and contrast. Finally, "it is argued" and "however" are most commonly used in persuasive writing. These samples are further explained on the next page to illustrate the vocabulary words most commonly used with these specific types of writing.

cause and Effect

As a result of people using their savings and borrowing money to buy more and more stocks, the price of stocks began to fall. Consequently, people got nervous and started selling their stock, and confidence in businesses fell.

compare and contrast

Both the forty-niners and the pioneers headed west, facing many challenges and hardships. In contrast to the forty-niners who were in search of gold, the pioneers were looking for land.

Persuasive

It is argued by educators that nightly homework is necessary for students to achieve good grades in school; however, I maintain that strong practice in school is all that is needed.

Organizing Text Structure

With content and its specific vocabulary, along with conventional sentence patterns, students gain the most support for their writing when they are given an overall structure from which to model their written pieces. Here is where mentor texts, or written examples that explicitly show a format or type of writing, are invaluable teaching tools. In a writing lesson, therefore, students aren't simply asked as an assignment to delineate the causes of the fall of the Roman Empire. They are tasked with examining and analyzing written models of causes and effects that help them structure their responses.

Including a visual representation of the textural structure of writing can be effective in the classroom. Researchers at Mid-continent Research for Education and Learning (McREL) have identified nine instructional strategies that are most likely to improve student achievement across all content areas and grade levels. One of the nine instructional strategies is *nonlinguistic representations*. It states, "Knowledge is stored in two forms: linguistic and visual. The more students use both forms in the classroom, the more opportunity they have to achieve. Recently, use of nonlinguistic representation has proven not only to stimulate but also to increase brain activity." Its applications include: "the use of physical models ... to represent information (Marzano, Pickering, and Pollock 2001).

Throughout this book, visual representations are included to display in your social studies classroom. These are referred to as Mobiles. Mobile 1 (page 26) illustrates the structure students should use when writing block comparison essays.

Mobile 1

Comparative Essay: Block Comparison

TOPIC

Introduction of subjects to be compared

Characteristics of the first subject

BODY

Second subject compared and contrasted to first subject

CONCLUSION

Summary of key points or final statement(s) on the topic

Model Lesson: Compare and Contrast

The rest of Chapter 2 gives step-by-step directions for a model AGO lesson. This lesson includes instructions for completing a compare-and-contrast writing assignment with students. The assignment asks students to compare and contrast the Senate and House of Representatives.

The first step is to answer organizing questions, such as:

1. What topic or unit of study will the writing lesson be a part of?

   - the two Houses of Congress in the legislative branch of the government

2. What do I want students to learn from the lesson and its writing task?

   - communicate their understandings of the similarities and differences between Senators and Representatives

   - use domain-specific vocabulary in their written pieces

   - use the language and text structure of comparative writing

3. What is the purpose of the writing or the genre, and which format are students using?

   - compare-and-contrast prose report

4. How will the lesson's key writing concepts be introduced to students?

   - I often present an example of a comparative text. The text is used to review (or to introduce) the elements of a comparative text with questions, such as these:

     - What do we notice about the introduction used in the text? Is it effective? Why or why not?

     - What are the subjects of the text? How are they introduced in the paper?

     - How are the subjects different? Similar?

     - What words are used in the text to compare? To contrast?

     - How is the text concluded? Is it effective? Why or why not?

After responding to the organizing questions, use the *AGO Teaching Plan* (Figure 2.2; reproducible on page 151) to organize the details for the lesson. The two figures on page 28 each include blank copies of the reproducibles as well as completed examples for this model compare-and-contrast lesson.

Figure 2.2 AGO Teaching Plan

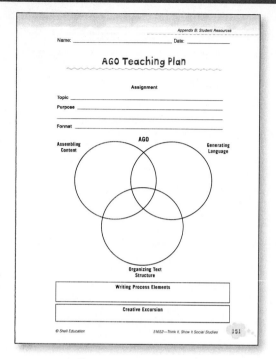

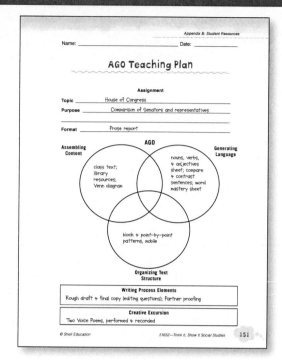

Blank Reproducible   Student Example

Once the planning stage is complete, prepare the content text for students by using the *Compare-and-Contrast Text Plan* (Figure 2.3; reproducible on page 152). This will provide students with the social studies content necessary to complete the writing assignment.

Figure 2.3 Compare-and-Contrast Text Plan

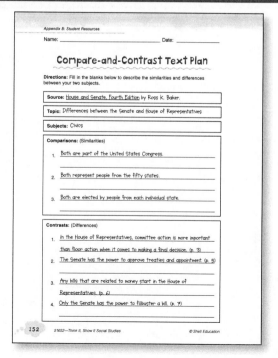

Blank Reproducible   Student Example

Figure 2.4, reproducible on page 153, is an example text created from the planning done on the *Compare-and-Contrast Text Plan*. Students are to read the text and fill in the comparisons between the Senate and House of Representatives with Venn diagrams. Then, they find and underline the words to compare and contrast in the text. Figure 2.5 is a sample Venn diagram.

Figure 2.4 Sample Compare-and-Contrast Text

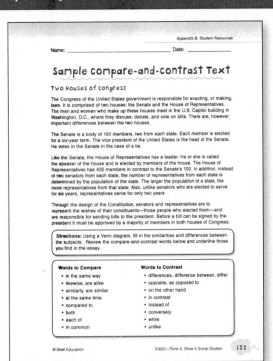

Figure 2.5 Sample Venn Diagram

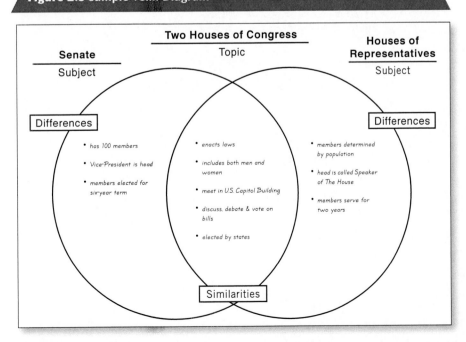

Model Lesson Step A – Assembling Content

The first step for students is to gather and assemble their content. A Venn diagram is one strategy for students to assemble content. Another strategy is to have students use the *Compare-and-Contrast Text Plan* (Figure 2.3; reproducible on page 152). Although it has limited lines for both the comparisons and contrasts, answers can be continued on the back or on additional sheets of paper. This sheet is most beneficial when students are doing close readings of a chapter or a section from their class texts or reference sources. They have the sheets next to them as they read to fill out as they discover relevant similarities and differences between their subjects. An important requirement with this process is that students record the page numbers of the information from sources. This reinforces the use of textual evidence.

After assembling the content but before writing the essay, give students the *Compare-and-Contrast Rubric* (Figure 2.6; reproducible on page 194) and have them add it to their Writer's Notebooks.

Figure 2.6 Compare-and-Contrast Rubric

Compare-and-Contrast Rubric

	10	5	1
Content	Includes similarities and differences of subjects that are accurate and complete. Where appropriate, specific, supporting details and examples are given. Contains no irrelevant information.	Information is generally accurate. Many of the similarities and differences between the subjects are given but not with a complete discussion. Lacks sufficient elaboration.	Lacks accurate and complete information of the similarities and differences of subjects. Possibly irrelevant information is included.
Organization and Structure	Introduction and conclusion are well written and effective. Paper follows one of the comparison patterns. Body paragraphs include topic sentences and follow logical progression of ideas. Transition words provide smooth movement from one idea to the next.	Paper has introduction and conclusion, but the body isn't clearly organized with one of the comparison patterns. Body paragraphs lack definitive topic sentences. Some transitions work, but the connections between other ideas are unclear.	Lacks or has poorly written introduction and/or conclusion. Paper doesn't follow one of the comparison patterns. There is an illogical presentation of ideas and/or weak transitions from one idea to the next.
Language	Correctly and accurately uses domain-specific and precise vocabulary. Includes compare-and-contrast sentences.	There is a limited use of domain-specific and precise vocabulary and compare-and-contrast sentences.	There is no use or inaccurate use of domain-specific vocabulary and compare-and-contrast sentences.
Grammar, Usage, Mechanics, and Spelling	Paper has only a few errors that do not distract or impede meaning.	There are several errors that potentially distract from the reading of the text.	Weak language skills impede the meaning. The writing is error-ridden.

Looking at the first criterion (content), this is a great opportunity to present a mini lesson on relevant versus irrelevant information (see below). According to the rubric, a score of 10 requires the following: "similarities and differences of subjects are accurate and complete. Where appropriate, specific, supporting details and examples are given. Contains no irrelevant information."

Model It!

We first discuss the purpose of the writing (comparative text), drawing from students' prior knowledge and coming to a consensus definition. Then, turn the conversation to the specific content and topic, in this case the differences between the House of Representatives and the Senate. Take random bits of information (both relevant and irrelevant) from the book and write them on the board. Discuss each with students and collectively determine which are relevant to the expressed purpose of the essay and which are not. Identify the relevant versus irrelevant data on the board.

Here is a sampling of information determined to be not relevant:

- The Senate is similar to the House of Lords in the parliamentary system.
- The first bicameral legislature in the colonies was the House of Burgesses.
- The system of checks and balances keeps any one branch from dominating the government.

Model Lesson Step G – Generating Language

The next step in the AGO model is for students to generate and learn the domain-specific language for their topic. During the study of Congress, students will be compiling lists of the nouns, verbs, and adjectives associated with the topic. These words will be used to complete *Nouns, Verbs, and Adjectives* (Figure 2.7; reproducible on page 180). Figure 2.7 on page 32 includes both the blank reproducible as well as a completed example for your reference. A helpful strategy is to have the geometric shapes featured on the sheet displayed on a bulletin board in the classroom. Those become references for students and can be used throughout the lesson. An extension of how to use the activity sheet is included in Chapter 6.

Figure 2.7 Nouns, Verbs, and Adjectives

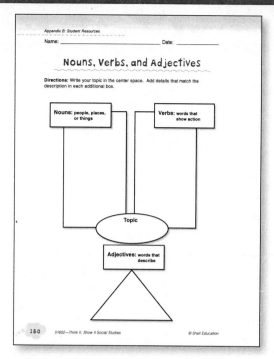

Blank Reproducible

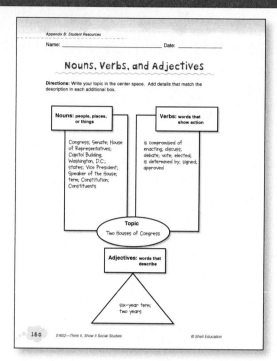

Student Example

In addition, students will complete *Word Mastery* (Figure 2.8; reproducible on page 182) for learning and understanding critical words about their topics. In general, have students use this sheet with the more abstract words (e.g., *comprised*, *enacting*). Figure 2.8 includes both a blank reproducible and a student example for your reference.

Figure 2.8 Word Mastery

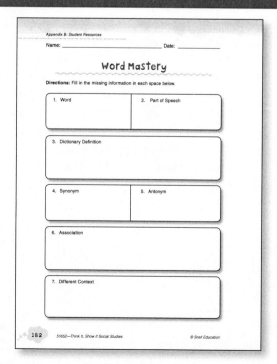

Blank Reproducible

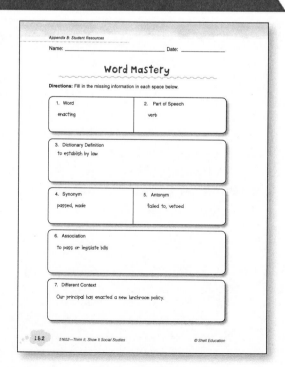

Student Example

Model Lesson Step O – Organizing Text Structures

The final stage in the AGO model is identifying and applying the correct language and text structure to best fit the type of writing. Mentor texts that can be included in the lesson are best suited in this section. Providing mentor texts gives students specific samples of the language and structure that is expected in their writing. To give students practice and to familiarize them with the language of comparisons, have them complete *Compare-and-Contrast Sentences* (Figure 2.9; reproducible on page 154). Using the content that they assembled, they practice writing compare-and-contrast sentences using words or phrases that compare and contrast. Figure 2.9 includes both the blank reproducible and a student example for your reference.

Figure 2.9 Compare-and-Contrast Sentences

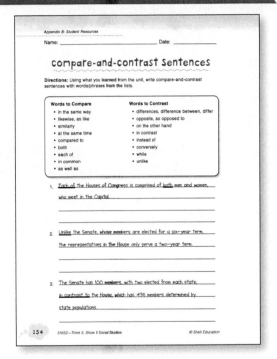

Blank Reproducible   Student Example

To examine and analyze the organization and different structures of comparative texts, use Mobiles 1 and 2. Mobile 1 on page 26 illustrates block comparison writing. Mobile 2 on page 35 illustrates point-by-point comparison writing. Also provided are annotated mentor texts, which model by example both the language and the structures of the different text types. After the introduction, the first half of a block comparison examines one of its subjects. The latter half is then a comparison of the similarities and differences between the two subjects. With a point-by-point comparison, individual comparisons are presented as matched pairs throughout the body of the essay.

Copies of both mobiles are available in the digital resources and can be reproduced and posted in your classroom or pasted into students' Writer's Notebooks. In class, introduce the mobiles and examine them with the appropriate mentor texts. Students will take notes and write summaries in their Writer's Notebooks. One strategy is to make the mobiles out of construction paper, laminate them, and hang them from a bulletin board to display as examples for students.

Included in Chapter 7 are copies of both the block and the point-by-point annotated and unannotated *Two Houses of Congress* texts (pages 120–123). Another way to use the block and point-by-point comparisons is with search-and-identify activities. Using Figure 2.10 (reproducible on page 155) type or post comparative texts for students to analyze.

Figure 2.10 Compare and Contrast: Search-and-Identify

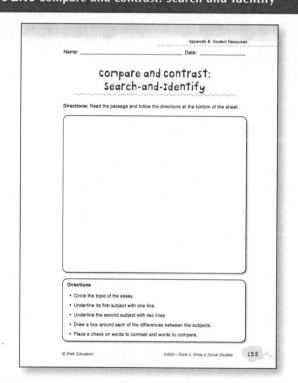

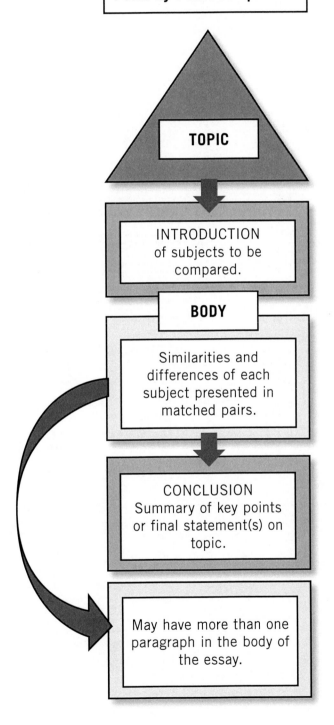

**Comparative Essay:
Point-by-Point Comparison**

TOPIC

INTRODUCTION
of subjects to be
compared.

BODY

Similarities and
differences of each
subject presented in
matched pairs.

CONCLUSION
Summary of key points
or final statement(s) on
topic.

May have more than one
paragraph in the body of
the essay.

Figure 2.11 Mentor Text Block Comparison

```
┌─────────────────────────┐
│  Comparative Essay:     │
│  Block Comparison       │
└─────────────────────────┘
```

TOPIC

INTRODUCTION of subjects to be compared.

Characteristics of the first subject.

BODY

Second subject is compared and contrasted to the first subject.

CONCLUSION Summary of key points or final statement(s) on topic.

Annotated Block comparison: Two Houses of congress

The Congress of the United States government is responsible for enacting*, or making, laws. It is comprised of* two houses: the Senate **[1st subject]** and the House of Representatives **[2nd subject]**. The men and women who make up these houses meet in the U.S. Capitol building in Washington, D.C., where they discuss, debate, and vote on bills. There are, however, important differences between the two houses **[topic sentence]**.

The Senate is a body of 100 members, two from each state. Each member is elected for a six-year term. The vice president of the United States is the head of the Senate. He votes in the Senate in the case of a tie.

Like **[words to compare]** the Senate, the House of Representatives has a leader **[similiarities between subjects]**. He or she is called the speaker of the house and is elected by members of the House **[difference between subjects]**. The House of Representatives has 435 members, in contrast **[words to contrast]** to the Senate's 100 **[difference between subjects]**. In addition, instead of two senators from each state **[difference between subjects]**, the number of representatives from each state is determined by the population of the state. The larger the population of a state, the more representatives from that state. Also unlike **[words to contrast]** senators, who are elected to serve for six years, representatives serve for only two years **[difference between subjects]**.

Through the design of the Constitution, senators and representatives are to represent the wishes of their constituents—those people who elected them—and are responsible for sending bills to the president. Before a bill can be signed by the president it must be approved by a majority of members in both houses of Congress.

*Working with new and more precise vocabulary: "enacting" & "is comprised of" (See *Word Mastery* sheet.)

Mentor Text: Block comparison

After the introduction of the subjects, the first half of the essay examines one of its subjects. The latter half is a comparison of the similarities and differences between the two subjects. A concluding paragraph is often used to complete the essay.

This mentor text demonstrates *topic* of the comparison essay, *subjects, words to compare,* and *words to contrast.*

Figure 2.12 Mentor Text Point-by-Point Comparison

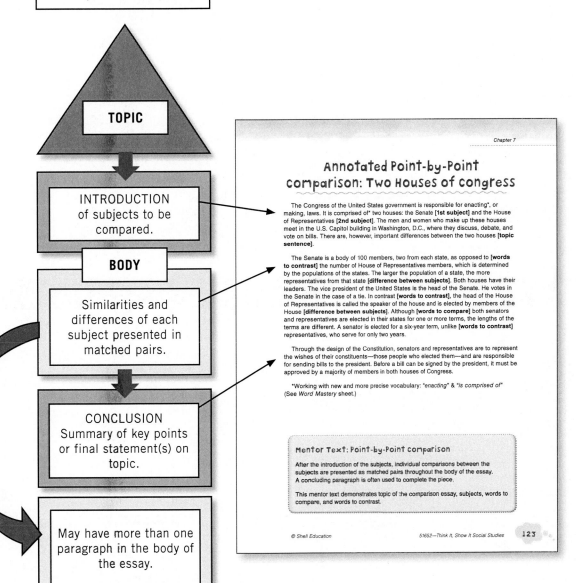

Comparative Essay:
Point-by-Point Comparison

TOPIC

INTRODUCTION
of subjects to be compared.

BODY

Similarities and differences of each subject presented in matched pairs.

CONCLUSION
Summary of key points or final statement(s) on topic.

May have more than one paragraph in the body of the essay.

Chapter 7

Annotated Point-by-Point comparison: Two Houses of congress

The Congress of the United States government is responsible for enacting*, or making, laws. It is comprised of* two houses: the Senate **[1st subject]** and the House of Representatives **[2nd subject]**. The men and women who make up these houses meet in the U.S. Capitol building in Washington, D.C., where they discuss, debate, and vote on bills. There are, however, important differences between the two houses **[topic sentence]**.

The Senate is a body of 100 members, two from each state, as opposed to **[words to contrast]** the number of House of Representatives members, which is determined by the populations of the states. The larger the population of a state, the more representatives from that state **[difference between subjects]**. Both houses have their leaders. The vice president of the United States is the head of the Senate. He votes in the Senate in the case of a tie. In contrast **[words to contrast]**, the head of the House of Representatives is called the speaker of the house and is elected by members of the House **[difference between subjects]**. Although **[words to compare]** both senators and representatives are elected in their states for one or more terms, the lengths of the terms are different. A senator is elected for a six-year term, unlike **[words to contrast]** representatives, who serve for only two years.

Through the design of the Constitution, senators and representatives are to represent the wishes of their constituents—those people who elected them—and are responsible for sending bills to the president. Before a bill can be signed by the president, it must be approved by a majority of members in both houses of Congress.

*Working with new and more precise vocabulary: "enacting" & "is comprised of" (See *Word Mastery* sheet.)

Mentor Text: Point-by-Point comparison

After the introduction of the subjects, individual comparisons between the subjects are presented as matched pairs throughout the body of the essay. A concluding paragraph is often used to complete the piece.

This mentor text demonstrates topic of the comparison essay, subjects, words to compare, and words to contrast.

© Shell Education   51652—Think It, Show It Social Studies   **123**

The Writing Process

After students complete the AGO plan, it is time to focus on the elements of the writing process that you will implement in the lesson. With an assignment such as this, have students write first drafts, use editing questions to edit their papers, and work with partners to partner proof their work before turning in final copies.

Creative Excursion

At this point, the lesson could be concluded, or you could choose to have a creative excursion as part of the lesson. Although not always used, look for possible creative extensions, or what will be referenced simply as *excursions*, in writing lessons. For example, with comparative writing, you can have students work in pairs to write and eventually perform two-voice poems. These excursions have students write poems with two first-person voices. The narration goes back and forth and in chorus together. *Two-Voice Poems* (Figure 2.13; reproducibles on pages 183–184) are a great way to creatively share comparisons. Figure 2.13 includes both a blank reproducible and an example from this lesson's study of Congress.

Figure 2.13 Two-Voice Poem

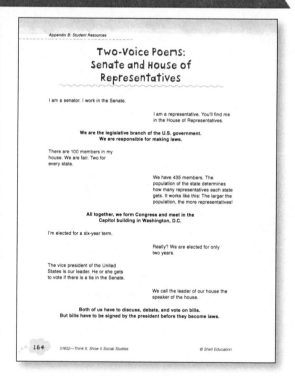

Blank Reproducible   Student Example

Conclusion

Comparing and contrasting is an essential skill taught and used in most social studies classrooms. It is a social studies skill that is universal at all grade levels, albeit at varying degrees of rigor. Having students write comparisons and contrasts can be done with many topics and units. Here is a small sampling of topics to compare and contrast:

- **Government and Civics: Citizenship**—Being a good, responsible citizen is important in a democracy. Compare the acts and behaviors of responsible citizenship with the acts and behaviors of what you consider poor citizenship.

- **Geography: Human Environment Interaction**—How do human beings change the environment? Pick a geographical area and compare what it is like today to how it was at an earlier time or era. Be sure to include in your paper how human beings contributed to the change.

- **History: Founding Fathers**—Pick two of our Founding Fathers and compare their contributions to U.S. history. What role did they play in the formation of our country?

- **Economics: Supply and Demand**—What is the difference between supply and demand? Compare the supply products of a person or group of people with those who demand the products.

Writing for Different Purposes

To help students understand the different purposes and types of writing that are important in social studies, I start by having them close their eyes and imagine their "dream cars."

If you had all the money you would ever need, what car would you have in your driveway? Think about what it would look like, how it would drive, how fast it could go, what technology it would have … Everything!

When they have fully visualized all of its details and are totally enthralled by their imagined dream cars, I say:

Now, drop the engine out. What do you have now?

After the chorus of moans, I go on to explain that they have, from all appearances, what look like fabulous cars. Each car has wheels, doors, and every high-tech, computerized, luxury option possible, but it has no engine and no power. It won't go anywhere. It won't take them anywhere. It will just sit in the driveway and rust. The same is true with writing. I go on to say:

You can have words on paper—even correctly spelled words. You can have indented your paragraphs properly and adhered to your margins and included a title. So now it looks like great writing, but writing has to have a motor. It has to be powered and have an objective. If it does not, it's simply words on paper without purpose. The words in any writing have to accomplish something such as describing an idea, explaining a procedure, or presenting a comparison of two or more subjects. Perhaps what the words need to do is to persuade readers to agree with your views about an issue. If they don't, it is like the car that just "looks" like a car: a piece of writing with no engine.

In the same way that the engine powers a car, it is the purpose that drives a piece of writing. This discussion, of course, is a lead-in to an examination of the different purposes of writing. In the previous chapter, compare and contrast was the purpose of writing used for the example lesson. Compare and contrast is one of six categories of writing that will be examined in this book. This chapter will examine the other five in greater detail.

Categories of Writing Purposes

- opinion, persuasive, and argumentative
- informative/explanatory
- narrative
- descriptive
- cause and effect
- compare and contrast

Opinion, Persuasive, and Argumentative

Opinion pieces are where a writer aims to share his or her opinion, relying on feelings and stating what he or she thinks and why. In a persuasive piece, the writer aims to convince or persuade the reader to agree with his or her perspective by blending facts with opinion. Only the writer's point of view is presented. Unlike persuasive writing, a formal argument addresses multiple sides of an issue. Writers aim to get readers to accept their sides by presenting claims and counterclaims. The piece relies on reasons and credible data that support the argument. Arguments are more formal and maintain objective third-person points of view.

Opinion Pieces

Opinion pieces will be an easy purpose for students to grasp, as the writing provides the reasons that support students' opinions. The organization of the opinion is key to success of this writing purpose. The student must be given the structure with which they build their opinion pieces. First, students must introduce the topics they are writing about. Then, they provide the reasons that support their opinions in the bodies of the texts. Finally, they should include closing statements to their opinion pieces. You can follow the steps of this pattern with beginning students: opinion sentence, reason sentences, and summary sentence.

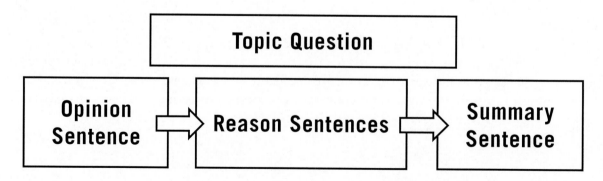

Opinion Sentence

Write an opening sentence clearly stating your opinion (what you think). Include key words from the topic question in your sentence. Use one of the sentence stems to start:

- I think ...
- I don't think ...
- I believe ...
- I don't believe ...
- In my opinion ...

Note: With advanced students, add these sentence stems:

- From my point of view ...
- I question whether ...
- I maintain that ...
- I (dis)agree with ...

Reason Sentences

Continue by writing two or more sentences with the reasons that support your opinion (why you think what you think). Use one transition (linking) word with each sentence:

- first
- second
- also
- next
- finally
- in addition

Note: With advanced students, have them write more than two sentences and give them these transition phrases to help them elaborate on their reasons:

- as an example
- for a case in point
- for instance
- in fact
- therefore
- despite
- on the other hand
- moreover
- besides
- furthermore

Summary Sentence

Finish by writing a sentence where you summarize the reasons for your opinion.

Note: More advanced students need to make sure that their summary sentences summarize and support the reasons given in the paper.

After reading a short article on Thomas Edison, a topic question could be: *In your opinion, what were the characteristics of Thomas Edison that helped make him a success?* The text on the following page is an example of a response:

> In my opinion, there were two characteristics that helped make Thomas Edison a success. First, his curiosity led him to start experimenting at a young age. As a boy, he set up a laboratory in a baggage car of a train he worked on, so he could experiment in his spare time. Second, he had many failures with his experiments, but he never gave up. His first patent in 1870 was not a success. Thomas's curiosity and the fact that he never gave up helped make him a success.

In the student sample above, notice that the student:

- included key words (*characteristics*, *made him a success*) from the topic question in the opinion sentence;
- used transition words (*first*, *second*) to sequence the reasons;
- supported the opinion with reasons; and
- summarized the reasons (*curiosity*; *never giving up*) in the concluding sentence.

As a culminating activity, have students color-code their paragraphs. With highlighters or colored pens, they should color their opinion sentences green; their reason/evidence sentences yellow; and their summary sentences red. In addition, they can circle all transition words and phrases. The *Student Opinion Paper Guide* (Figure 3.1; reproducible on page 156) serves as a guiding activity for students writing opinion pieces. Figure 3.1 includes a blank reproducibles as well as a student example.

Figure 3.1 Student Opinion Paper Guide

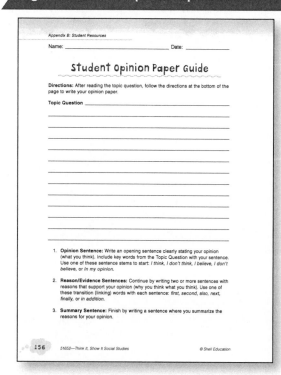

Blank Reproducible

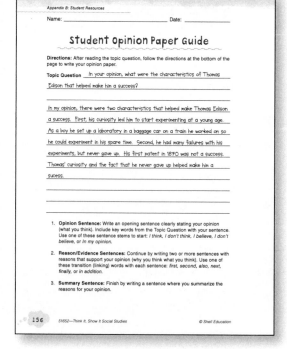

Student Example

Persuasive Pieces

As students mature with the writing they complete in social studies, they move beyond simple opinion paragraphs to longer persuasive pieces. Where opinion papers rely solely on the writer's opinions and feelings, persuasion texts blend their opinions with facts to convince readers to agree. Opinions evolve into the writer's positions. The *Topic, Issue, and Position Statement Planning Grid* activity sheet (Figure 3.2; reproducible on page 157) directs students to do four things:

1. State the topic.

2. Identify the issue and his or her position on the given issue.

3. Select relevant background information.

4. Develop reasons to support the position.

Figure 3.2 Topic, Issue, and Position Statement Planning Grid

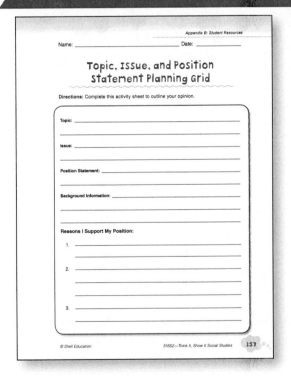

Blank Reproducible

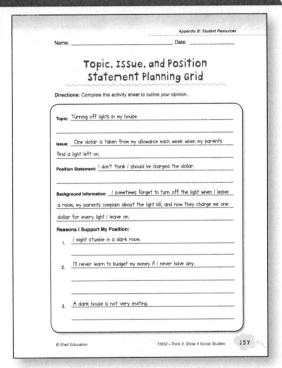

Student Example

Model It!

While studying rules and laws along with Kathleen Krull's *A Kids' Guide to America's Bill of Rights: Curfews, Censorship, and the 100-Pound Giant*, students were prompted to think about all the rules of community life: home, school, neighborhood, and so much more. Then, they selected one of the rules they have at home and took a position against it. Figure 3.3 is an example of an *Unannotated Persuasive Letter Mentor Text* (page 126).

Figure 3.3 Unannotated Persuasive Letter: House Rules

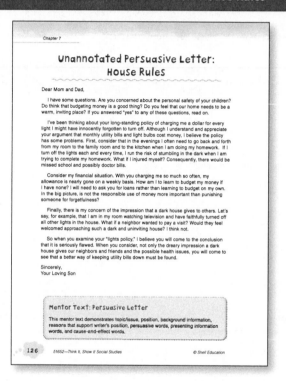

After the students filled out their sheets, they then wrote letters to their parents in attempts to persuade them regarding the rules. (Parents were also invited to write responses.)

To help support the composition of the letters, students use the *How to Structure a Persuasive Essay* sheet (Figure 3.4; reproducible on page 158), from which they can pick key persuasive words and phrases.

Figure 3.4 How to Structure a Persuasive Essay

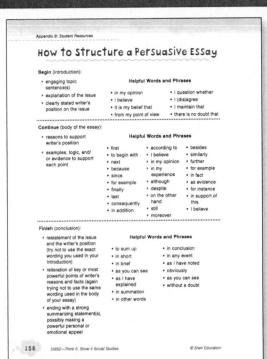

Using "persuasive sentence stems," students pick words and phrases to help them write persuasive sentences.

Persuasive Sentence Stems

- I realize you _____ (*believe, feel, maintain, want, favor, support, argue, make the case/point*) ...

- I understand you _____ (*believe, feel, maintain, want, favor, support, argue, make the case/point*) ...

- Even though you _____ (*believe, feel, maintain, want, favor, support, argue, make the case/point*) ...

- Although you _____ (*believe, feel, maintain, want, favor, support, argue, make the case/point*) ...

- _____ (*but, yet, however*) I question _____ (*on the other hand, nevertheless*) ...

Topic Sentences

With both opinion papers and persuasive pieces, students can practice effective ways to begin their paragraphs. Maureen E. Auman, in a program called *Step Up to Writing*, has formulated a series of methods or patterns for writing topic sentences. Four of them are adapted here. These are particularly helpful when students write opinion papers and shorter persuasive pieces. The patterns are:

- number statements
- topic/opinion statements or issue/position statements
- "however" statements
- *and*, *but*, and *or* statements

Number Statements

A number statement is an opening sentence that contains a number word or phrase. These words might be used in number statements:

- a couple of
- a few
- a number of
- many
- numerous

- several
- ten
- three
- two
- various

Example Number Sentences

- There are *numerous* ways in which humans interact with the environment.
- Greece was home to *various* city-states.
- *Two* Founding Fathers had great influence over the beginnings of America.
- Trade is *one* of the *many* reasons countries cooperate.
- *Two* important characteristics that Thomas Edison had that made him a success were persistence and love of knowledge.
- There are *several* things that I would like you to consider regarding our long-standing rule and consequences for not turning lights off.

Topic/Opinion Statements

A topic/opinion statement is a sentence that begins with a preposition or prepositional phrase. Here are examples of different prepositions and prepositional phrases students can use in their writing:

- although
- as
- as long as
- as soon as
- because
- before

- even though
- even while
- if after
- since
- unless

- until
- when
- whenever
- whether
- while

After introducing the preposition and prepositional phrase, a student can draw the connection to his or her topic. The topic of the paper is given first and followed by a comma. Then, the writer's opinion is given.

Example Topic/Opinion Statements

- *Before* Thomas Edison became a success as an inventor, he had many personal characteristics that helped him.

- *Even though* Congress can pass laws, the president can still veto them.

- *Since* the Industrial Revolution, lifestyles have changed completely.

- *After* being purchased from the French, the Louisiana Territory needed to be explored.

- *As* the Nineteenth Amendment was added to the Constitution, voting rights were finally granted to women.

Issue/Position Statements

Like the topic/opinion statement, the issue/position statement begins with a preposition or prepositional phrase. Issue/position statements are generally introduced to advanced students. These are some commonly used issue/position statements:

- after
- although
- as
- as long as
- as soon as
- because

- before
- even though
- even while
- if
- since
- unless

- until
- when
- whenever
- whether
- while

After introducing the preposition and prepositional phrase, a student should draw the connection to his or her topic. It should be written as a dependent clause and then present the issue, followed with a comma. Then, the writer's position is stated as an independent clause.

Example Issue/Position Statements

- *Although* there were many important battles in the Revolutionary War, one of the most famous is the Battle of Bunker Hill.

- *Even though* globalization has many benefits, it also comes with a cost.

- *While* the Greeks and Romans were both European, their differences outweighed their similarities.

- *Even while* the president is in charge of the country, there are still limits on what he can do.

"However" Statements

These are generally introduced to more advanced students. While the issue/position statement begins with a preposition or prepositional phrase, the *however* statement has a conjunctive adverb in the middle of the sentence. The sentence begins with the issue stated as an independent clause and is followed by a semicolon. After the issue is stated, the conjunctive adverb *however* is inserted and followed by a comma. Then, the second part of the sentence is an independent clause stating the position of the writer. For example: *I know that for our home to be safe and comfortable, we need rules;* however, *one of our rules needs to be amended.*

With the *however* statement, other conjunctive adverbs can be used in place of the word *however.* These are example conjunctive adverbs that can be used:

- as a result
- consequently
- furthermore
- in fact
- instead

- meanwhile
- nevertheless
- otherwise
- still
- therefore

Example "However" Statements

- There are many famous French icons; *however*, the most recognizable is the Eiffel Tower.

- Deforestation has damaging ecological effects; *therefore*, action needs to be taken.

- Hammurabi's Code was full of violent punishments; *nevertheless*, it was a revolutionary legal system.

- Alexander conquered the Persians and had many impressive accomplishments; *as a result*, he is known as "Alexander the Great."

And, But, and *Or* Statements

These are generally introduced to older students. *And, but,* and *or* statements use coordinating conjunctions remembered by students with the acronym FANBOYS (for, and, nor, but, or, yet, so). Similar to *however* statements, the *and, but,* and *or* statements begin with the issue stated as an independent clause. It is followed with a comma. One of the FANBOYS words is then inserted, and the writer's position is written as an independent clause.

Example *And, But,* and *Or* Statements

- The United States has had many great leaders, *but* the best was Abraham Lincoln.

- Some geographic regions feature harsh climates, *yet* people have managed to find ways to live there.

- People need a variety of goods and services on a daily basis, *and* if it weren't for local government, these needs wouldn't be met.

- One area might not produce something on its own, *so* there will always be a need for trade.

Argumentative Pieces

Formal arguments share much of the same concepts and features as opinion papers and persuasive texts: topics, opinions, points of view, issues, positions, arguments, and counter arguments. Along with these, formal arguments introduce the concepts of claims and counterclaims. The formal argument is representative of the type of academic writing expected of college-and career-ready, twenty-first century students.

The elements of an argument include:

- Present a claim(s) about a topic or an issue.

- Differentiate the claim(s) from opposing claims.

- Logically arrange the evidence.

- Support the claim(s) with logical reasoning and relevant, accurate data.

- Evidence should demonstrate an understanding of the topic or text.

- Use and cite credible sources.

- Use words, phrases, and clauses to create cohesion.

- Clarify the differences between the claim(s), counterclaim(s), reason(s), and evidence.

- Always use an academic, formal style.

- In the conclusion, incorporate a section that supports the argument being presented.

The foundation of an effective argument is the anticipation of the reasons for an opposing position or point of view. Students can map out the points of their counterclaims with the *Opposing Reasons/Your Argument Planning Sheet* (Figure 3.5; reproducible on page 159).

Figure 3.5 Opposing Reasons/Your Argument Planning Sheet

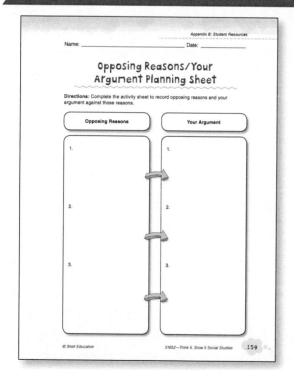

Blank Reproducible

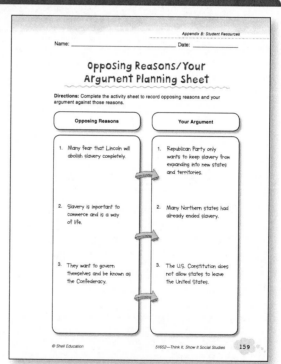

Student Example

Using the sheet to plan and research the basis of their arguments, students are given (or select) topics or issues. They need to determine their positions on the issues. On the left side of the sheet, they determine three possible counterclaims (or more, if needed) to their positions. Directly across from each opposing reason, they formulate and write their counterclaims. Figure 3.5 includes an example using the topic of the 1861 secession of the Southern states upon the election of Abraham Lincoln. For this particular assignment, students were to take positions as if they were living at that time.

From the *Opposing Reasons/Your Argument Planning Sheet* students generated the following response:

> *The Republican Party argued that the South's fear that Lincoln was going to abolish slavery and that they would lose their commerce and way of life was completely unfounded. The North only wanted to keep slavery from expanding into the new states and territories. They had already ended slavery and didn't want it in new states. Furthermore, they maintained that while the South wanted to secede and become a separate country known as the Confederacy, the U.S. Constitution did not allow states to separate from the Union.*

Argument T

The *Argument T-Chart* activity sheet (Figure 3.6; reproducible on page 160) functions much like the *Opposing Reasons/Your Argument Sheet*. On it, students map out the basis of their formal arguments. With this sheet, students approach assembling the bodies of their arguments as if they were preparing for a class debate (pros and cons). They first record the topics, issues, and their positions at the top of the sheet. Then, on the left side, they write the alternate or opposing claims to their positions. On the right side, they record their rebuttals.

Figure 3.6 Argument T-Chart

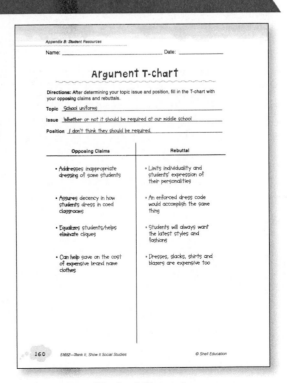

Blank Reproducible   Student Example

Introduction, Body, and Conclusion

The three structural blocks of an argument are the introduction, the body of the argument, and the conclusion. Mobile 4 (reproducible on page 191) is a visual representation of this structure.

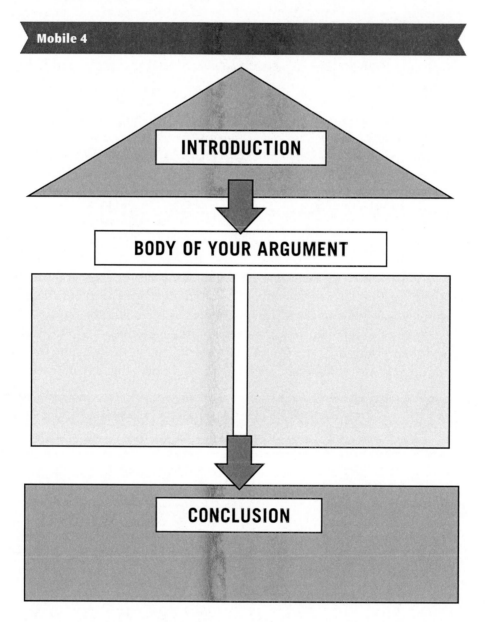

Mobile 4

INTRODUCTION

BODY OF YOUR ARGUMENT

CONCLUSION

Introduction

The introduction provides the context of what students are arguing in their papers. This should consist of an introduction to the topic or issue, an acknowledgement of the counterclaim(s), and a thesis statement expressing the writer's position. It is important to note that persuasive essays can be written in informal, conversational tones. With formal arguments, however, formal, academic style of writing is expected. This writing is free of slang, trite expressions, abbreviations, symbols, email/text shortcut language, contractions, and the use of the personal pronoun *I*. With formal writing, the writer does not speak directly to the reader, but rather maintains an objective third-person point of view.

Body of the Argument

There are three elements critical to a formal argument: opposing claims or views, rebuttals, and support statements. Students can structure these in the body of their papers by following one of two patterns: point-by-point or opposition/rebuttal. Figure 3.7 (reproducibles on pages 128 and 130) includes student examples of each type of argument. Pages 56–57 show visual models (Mobiles 5 and 6) of the two argument patterns, point-by-point and opposition/rebuttal.

- **Point-by-Point:** After the introduction, one opposing claim is given with the rebuttal following. Then, a second opposing claim is given followed by its rebuttal, and so on.

- **Opposition/Rebuttal:** After the introduction, all the opposing claims are explained and summarized before the writer presents a complete rebuttal.

Figure 3.7 Point-by-Point and Opposition/Rebuttal Argument Student Examples

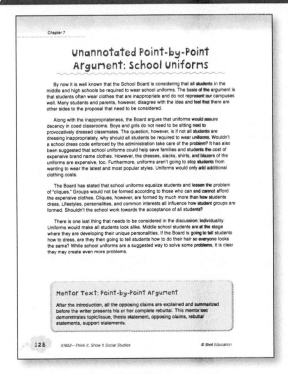

Point-by-Point Argument

Opposition/Rebuttal Argument

Mobile 5 Patterns of Argument

POINT by POINT

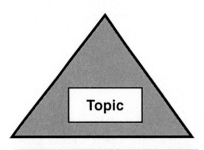

Topic

INTRODUCTION
Thesis Statement

OPPOSING
CLAIM AND
YOUR
REBUTTAL

OPPOSING
CLAIM AND
YOUR
REBUTTAL

OPPOSING
CLAIM AND
YOUR
REBUTTAL

CONCLUSION

Mobile 6 Patterns of Argument

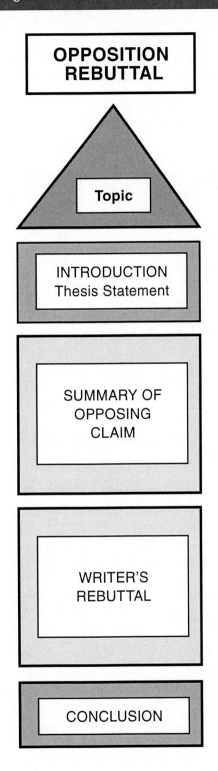

Conclusion

A conclusion acts as a summation of the student's argument. It brings the argument full circle. Often, a writer saves what he or she believes to be the strongest personal or emotional appeal for the conclusion. Typically included is a brief restatement of the writer's position and rebuttal, all while acknowledging opposing claims or points.

Figure 3.8 (reproducible on page 195) shows an *Argument Rubric*, which guides students in their work. In addition, annotated and unannotated mentor texts for both the point-by-point and opposition/rebuttal argument patterns are included in Chapter 7.

Figure 3.8 Argument Rubric

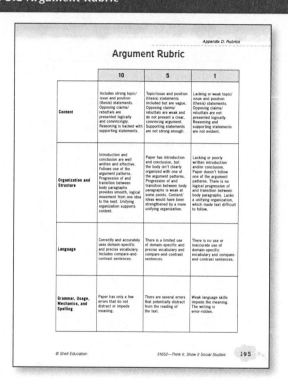

Informative/Explanatory

To state it as succinctly as possible: informative/explanatory writing conveys information accurately. Its accurately conveyed information may examine a topic, explain a process, an idea, or a concept, or demonstrate an understanding of why events occur or have occurred.

Four basic developmental goals for students when writing informative/explanatory texts are to:

- clearly introduce the topic and its context
- develop and organize relevant facts, details, and information
- use domain-specific vocabulary in an academic writing style
- produce coherent writing appropriate to the task, purpose, and audience

Organizing and Writing a Paragraph

Providing students with the structure of a paragraph is just as important as providing them a structure for an entire paper. In the same way as the other mobiles presented in this book, the paragraph mobile gives the beginning students a visual representation of the elements of a simple explanatory paragraph (Mobile 7; reproducible on page 192). Students should be told that although the mobile shows only two pieces of information and each with one detail, it is not limited to that. Using the mobile shapes, students understand that they may have more than two pieces of information. Some pieces of information may have only one supporting detail while others may have more.

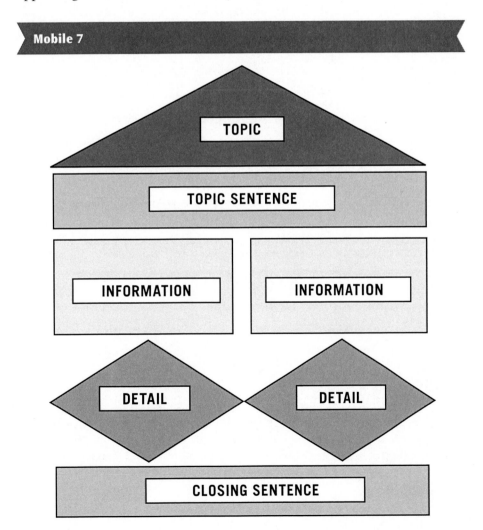

Mobile 7

TOPIC

TOPIC SENTENCE

INFORMATION   INFORMATION

DETAIL   DETAIL

CLOSING SENTENCE

The shapes on the mobile can be incorporated into the webs that students draw on their own papers or use with *Explanatory Text Planning Web* (Figure 3.9; reproducible on page 161). Figure 3.9 includes both a blank reproducible and a student example.

Figure 3.9 Explanatory Text Planning Web

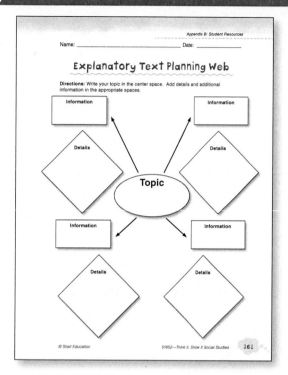
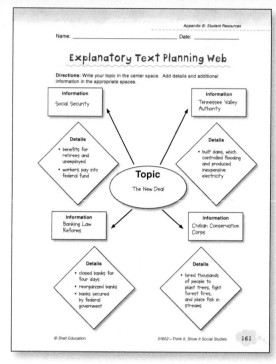

Blank Reproducible   Student Example

As an example, in discussions centered on community services, students identified four places where community services are found: fire departments, hospitals, police departments, and schools. With each one, they then added detail diamonds.

- fire departments—save our homes and buildings from fires

- hospitals—take care of us when we are hurt or sick

- police departments—protect us from crime

- schools—where we learn

Students also use the shapes with the *Explanatory Text Planning Chart* activity sheet (Figure 3.10; reproducible on page 162). On this sheet, they identify two pieces of information and list as many details as they can under each. The different shapes of the mobiles can also become a color code for writing. Students can highlight information sentences in yellow and supporting details in red. Figure 3.10 includes the blank reproducible and a student example.

Figure 3.10 Explanatory Text Planning Chart

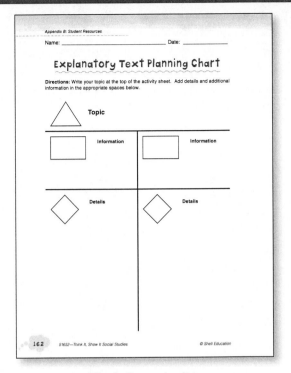

Blank Reproducible

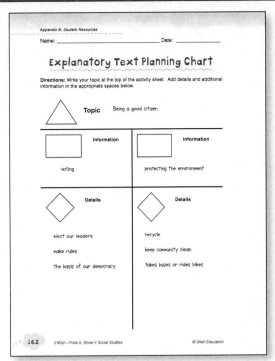

Student Example

Below is an example of student writing based on the *Explanatory Text Planning Chart* for an informative/explanatory piece on good citizenship. Given the topic "being a good citizen," the student first identified two characteristics: good citizens vote, and good citizens protect the environment. Then, underneath each of the information boxes, the student listed supporting details.

- **voting:** elect our leaders; make rules; the basis of our democracy

- **protecting the environment:** recycle; keep our community clean; take buses or ride bikes

Being a Good Citizen

Of the many characteristics of good citizenship, two are the most important. First, a good citizen needs to vote in elections. Voting is part of our democracy and how we elect our leaders. Our leaders make our laws. Second, it is important that good citizens protect our environment. They must recycle materials that can be recycled. They also need to keep our communities clean. Helping to keep our parks and neighborhoods clean is being a good citizen. Taking buses or riding bikes to help keep our air clean is another characteristic of a good citizen. Good citizens help make the country a better place to live.

Reports and Document-Based Questions Essays

In a most basic way, the paragraph mobile that is used with beginning students presents the developmental groundwork for the research reports and document-based questions essays required of advanced students. Topic sentences expand into introductions to become thesis statements. Information and detail sentences grow into paragraphs with main ideas supported with facts, definitions, details, quotations, and other information and/or examples. Concluding sentences transform into conclusion paragraphs that reiterate and sum up thesis statements.

Research Reports

Reports are generally shorter in length and scope than document-based questions essays. They present and summarize the findings of the student (or group of students). Stemming from an inquiry into or examination of a topic, reports solidify students' understanding. Finally, unlike opinion papers and persuasive pieces, research reports are compilations of objective research written without the writer's personal views or reactions to the topic.

In guiding students through the writing, start with these overlapping tasks. Essentially, the entry tickets indicate that they can now proceed and write their reports.

- select a topic
- narrow down the scope of a topic to what can be thoroughly covered
- during research, choose relevant information from both primary and secondary sources applicable to the historical context, scope, and focus of the report
- group information into major points or areas
- determine the main idea of the report

Then, students write the information on index cards. Once completed, this is then presented as an *Entry Ticket*. Figure 3.11 is an example of a completed *Entry Ticket* index card.

Figure 3.11 Entry Ticket

Entry ticket

My report is about ___the New Deal___ (topic).

___4___ (number) major points or areas about my topic are

1. ___Tennessee Valley Authority___
2. ___Social Security___
3. ___Banking law reforms___
4. ___Civil Conservation Corps___

The main idea of my report will be ___about the aims and goals of President Roosevelt's programs to restore the economy from the Great Depression.___

My source(s) for the report is/are

1. ___PBS's American Experience: Surviving the Dust Bowl___
2. ___Online article about the Great New Deal___

Figure 3.12 Explanatory Text Planning Web Student Sample

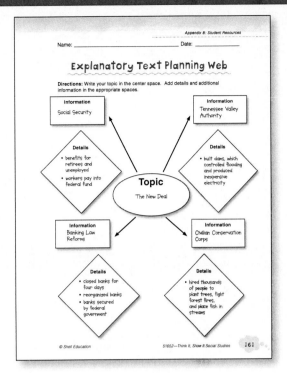

Student Example

Students may choose to use the shapes and structure of the *Explanatory Text Planning Web* (Figure 3.12, reproducible on page 161) to gather and begin to organize their information and supporting details. Figure 3.12 includes a student example of research on the New Deal.

From their report entry tickets, students begin to write their reports with these tasks:

- avoiding the pitfalls of plagiarism

- developing a thesis statement

- organizing the report in a meaningful, cohesive text with smooth transitions between ideas and paragraphs

Their reports are structured as an introduction, a body, and a conclusion. Statistics, quotations, or compelling statements are some of the different ways students may want to introduce their reports. Essential elements of an introduction are: a clear topic, the historical context of the topic, and a thesis statement. For the body of the writing, the general rule of thumb is that there is one paragraph for each major point or area of the report. Elaboration for each point or area comes from researched information and facts. There needs to be smooth, meaningful transitions between ideas and paragraphs. The conclusion includes a reiteration of the thesis statement and a reconnection to, or summation of, the historical context of the topic.

Transition Words

A secondary skill in writing reports, as well as in most formats of writing, is the use of transition words. Transition words function as links, connecting one idea to another idea, one sentence to another sentence, or one paragraph to another paragraph. In fact, transition words are often called *linking words and phrases*. Teaching students how to use them effectively helps them better organize the ideas and information in their reports. It also greatly improves the fluency and sentence variety of their writing pieces.

First, it is helpful for students to have a list of transition words to refer to as they write. *Pick a Great Combination of Transition Words* (Figure 3.13; reproducible on page 163) is a list for students to keep in their Writer's Notebooks. The words are separated into columns indicating which are useful in the beginning of a series of ideas, which are useful in the middle, and which announce the end of a series.

Figure 3.13 Pick a Great Combination of Transition Words

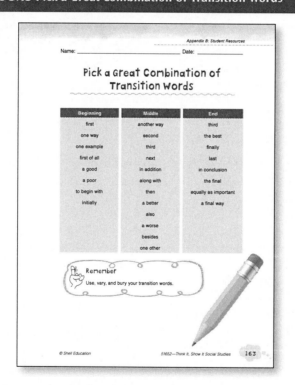

Second, students need to "use, vary, and bury" these transition words. Along with selecting words from the list, they should try to vary the ones they pick. In other words, students will vary the transitions instead of starting every new idea with the obvious word choices such as *also* or *next*. Additionally, there is a tendency to use transition words at the beginning of a sentence. This is a good opportunity to teach students to "bury" some of them. This simply means putting the transition words inside the sentences.

Vary Transition Words

- *To begin with*, to prevent people from continuing to withdraw more money from the banks, President Roosevelt …

- *Next*, he had to sign into law …

- *Another* project Roosevelt began in 1935 …

Bury Transition Words

- Roosevelt's Civilian Conservation Corps Act *also* gave jobs to three million young men.

The *Research Report Rubric* (Figure 3.14; reproducible on page 196) is a rubric to use with students when evaluating their writing. Along with a students' guide to writing research reports for their Writer's Notebooks, there is a mentor text, *Research Report: New Deal*, included in Chapter 7 (page 132).

Figure 3.14 Research Report Rubric

Appendix D: Rubrics

Research Report Rubric

	10	5	1
Content	Information, facts, concrete details, quotations, or other examples are evident and relevant to the context of the paper. Extensive and applicable research is clear.	Information, facts, concrete details, quotations, or other examples are evident but not always relevant to the text. Better research would have strengthened the paper.	Lacks relevant information, facts, concrete details, quotations, or other examples. Little or no research is evident.
Organization and Structure	Introduction and conclusion are well written and effective. Organized to present a cohesive connection between ideas or information. There is a smooth, logical movement from one idea to the next. Overall unifying organization evident and effective.	Paper has introduction and conclusion, but the body isn't effectively organized. Progression of transition between ideas or information is weak at some points. Content/ideas would have been strengthened by a more unifying organization.	Lacking or poorly written introduction and/or conclusion. Paper doesn't present a cohesive connection between ideas or information. Lack of a unifying organization makes the text difficult or impossible to follow.
Language	Correctly and accurately uses formal/academic language, domain-specific vocabulary, and precise wording.	Could improve use of formal/academic language, domain-specific vocabulary, and precise wording.	No use or inaccurate use of formal/academic language, domain-specific vocabulary, and precise wording.
Grammar, Usage, Mechanics, and Spelling	Paper has only a few errors that do not distract or impede meaning.	There are several errors that potentially distract from the reading of the text.	Weak language skills impede the meaning. The writing is error-ridden.

196   51652—Think It, Show It Social Studies   © Shell Education

Document-Based Question Essays: Primary and Secondary Sources

Essays written in response to document-based questions (DBQs) require students to work with historical sources in multiple forms. They challenge students to interpret these primary and secondary sources while applying their understanding of history to support a thesis.

These are examples of common historical sources:

- charts/graphs
- diaries
- government documents
- historians' accounts
- letters

- maps
- newspaper articles
- paintings
- photographs
- political cartoons

Model It!

Explain to students that document-based questions have two parts. Provide students with "scaffolding questions." With these, they are asked to answer one or two questions about each of the documents presented. In most cases, a short narrative of the historical context of the documents is also given. Answering the scaffolding questions necessitates that students interpret data and determine main ideas or points of view communicated by the documents.

The following are some example scaffolding questions for sources about commonly taught topics:

Charts/Graphs

What does the first chart indicate about the ethnic composition of the United States?

What does the second chart show about the changing ethnic composition in the United States?

Diaries

From this diary entry, what were the experiences of this Civil War soldier?

How do you think the writer feels about his decision to join the Confederacy?

Government Documents

What aspects have remained the same about the Constitution since the very beginning?

How did the Bill of Rights change the Constitution?

Historians' Accounts

What resources were available to the colonists?

How did the colonists utilize these resources?

Letters

What do the letters say about the relationship of enslaved people and their ownerss?

From the letters, what was the writers' motivation to try to escape?

Maps

What route did Lewis and Clark take west?

What were the different territories they traveled through?

Newspaper Article

How does the article describe the incident in Serbia?

For what reasons was this incident related to the beginning of World War I?

Paintings

For what reasons was this painting created?

How was the artist related to the subject of the painting?

Photographs

Based on the photograph, how do people travel in a rainforest?

What materials do they use to make travel possible?

Political Cartoons

According to the cartoon, what is the concern of developing countries?

What interpretation do you have about how developing nations feel about their situation?

Following the document and the scaffolding questions, students are presented with an essay question. In some cases, the essay question has more than one part. Moving beyond simply quoting or paraphrasing the document, students are to use the documents as evidence in support of their theses.

Example 1

Historical context: The struggle for equal rights for African Americans has been long and difficult. Beginning in the 1950s, the fight for equality gained momentum. This struggle for equality is known as the modern civil rights movement.

Essay Question: With the information from the documents and your knowledge of social studies, discuss:

- In what ways have African Americans been denied equal rights?

- What methods have individuals, groups, and/or the government used to deal with the inequalities faced by African Americans?

Example 2

Historical Context: The United States is a nation of immigrants. For a variety of reasons, groups of people from foreign lands left their native countries and relocated in the United States. Many of these immigrants faced hardships after they arrived in America.

Essay Question: With the information from the documents and your knowledge of social studies, discuss:

- For what reasons did immigrants come to the United States?

- What hardships did they face after arriving?

Students learn to use the following steps to write document-based question essay, which should be included in students' Writer's Notebooks. Have students copy the following into their notebooks:

Writing Document-Based Questions Essays

1. Read the essay question(s) carefully. Circle key concept(s).

    Essay Question: With the information from the documents and your knowledge of social studies, <u>discuss</u>:

    - In what ways have African Americans been denied equal rights?

    - What methods have individuals, groups, and/or the government used to deal with the inequalities faced by African Americans?

2. Underline the specific words as to what the question is asking you to do. Notice words such as *describe, discuss, explain,* and/or *show.*

    - Describe—to illustrate or depict something in words

    - Discuss—to write about something in detail using observations, facts, and/or reasoning

- Explain—to make plain or understandable; to account for; to give reasons for or causes of; to show the development of

- Show—to point out; to set forth clearly a position or idea by stating it and giving evidence to support it

3. Review your grading rubric. (A reproducible is included on page 197.)

4. Return to the documents, and review your answers to their questions.

5. Think about what you know about the topic of the documents and the essay question.

Provide students with the following graphic organizers to help them at each stage of their document-based question response. The first step is preparing their theses. To help formulate a thesis, use *Thesis Web* (Figure 3.15; reproducible on page 164). The web will help students organize ideas or information and its supporting evidence. Let students know they can add circles as needed. Figure 3.15 includes both a blank reproducible and a student example.

Figure 3.15 Thesis Web

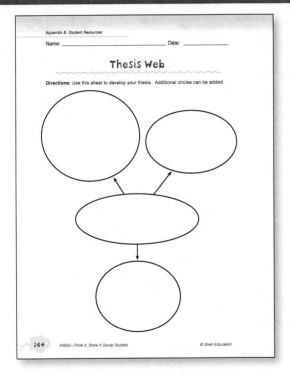

Blank Reproducible

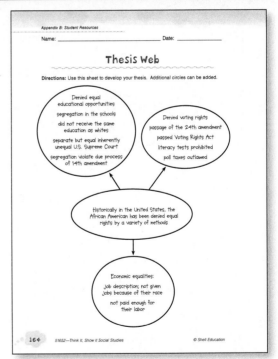

Student Example

After completing the *Thesis Web*, it is time to outline the rest of the essay. The elements of a *Five Paragraph Essay* (Figure 3.16; reproducible on page 193) will help students structure their essays. Remind them that their essays should have at least two body paragraphs but can have more than three. They should use the *Five Paragraph Essay* activity sheet to organize their writing.

Figure 3.16 Five Paragraph Essay

INTRODUCTION

Uses essay question for main idea; gives historical context; presents thesis statement; and makes reference to topics of body paragraphs.

BODY PARAGRAPH # 1

Begins with a topic sentence; presents and cites evidence from documents and social studies knowledge; and has smooth and effective transition between ideas.

BODY PARAGRAPH # 2

Begins with a topic sentence; presents and cites evidence from documents and social studies knowledge; and has smooth and effective transition between ideas.

BODY PARAGRAPH # 3

Begins with a topic sentence; presents and cites evidence from documents and social studies knowledge; and has smooth and effective transition between ideas.

CONCLUSION

Briefly reiterates historical context and essay question; sums up main idea; uses restated thesis statement to conclude essay.

Once the thesis is strong and the essay has been organized, the actual writing takes place. After the essay has been completed (a first draft, if you will) students need to edit and proofread their work. To help guide students with editing and proofreading, provide them with the following questions:

Proofreading/Editing Guiding Questions

- Have I written it with a formal, academic style?

- Have I been sure not to use the words "I" or "you"?

- Where needed, have I correctly cited the documents?

- Have I checked for complete sentences and corrected any sentence fragments?

- Have I used punctuation correctly?

- Have I double-checked my spelling?

A final note regarding citations with reports and document-based questions essays: Follow the expectations of the district's curriculum guidelines. These will address at what grade level students are expected to use either APA or MLA citations. In general, with reports written by third- through fifth-grade students, expect books, articles, videos, or online materials to be referenced by title at the end of the report. They do not need to footnote the references within the text. When sixth- through eighth-grade students create document-based questions essays, they will need to cite in the text from which document or source they attained critical information.

Narrative

There are endless possibilities for which students can write narratives in social studies. The underlying structure of a narrative is a beginning, a middle, and an end. A narrative centers on a character or characters, has a setting, and involves a plot of some sort. As part of social studies curriculum, writing narratives offers students opportunities to creatively demonstrate their knowledge of living and historical individuals, current and past events or issues, geographical regions, economic causes and effects, and the ins and outs of governments, both past and present.

In addition, narratives help students practice and refine language arts skills, such as:

- writing in first or third person

- leads and resolutions

- plotting and sequencing of story events

- use of dialogue

- descriptive words

Sample Narratives

Writing a narrative is really about telling a story. A narrative is told from a specific point of view. Many times, it is the point of view of the author. This is much more descriptive writing, so word choice and use of vocabulary can be critical elements to writing good narratives. There are six types of narratives:

- single historical event stories
- personification stories
- imagined conversation stories
- different perspective stories
- "life in" stories
- firsthand reporting stories

Single historical event stories: Single historical event stories are where students take single events from the life of historical figures and retell them in first-person narratives as if the writers were the chosen historical figures.

Sample Single Historical Event Stories

- General Robert E. Lee's surrender at the Appomattox Court House: *I remember the day as if it were yesterday.*

- a passenger on the Mayflower: *You can only imagine how I felt when, as a child, my parents told me that we would be leaving England on a ship.*

- Lewis and Clark reaching the Pacific: *After all the miles that seemed to never end, we reached the water.*

- a citizen in ancient Athens: *I was brushed out of the way by students rushing off to their classes with Plato at The Academy.*

- Marco Polo arriving in Asia: *There were immediately so many things different about this place that I had never seen before.*

Personification stories: Personification is when the qualities of a person are assigned to something that isn't human. Students can use the factual elements of topics and personify them as first person narratives.

Sample Personification Stories

- Seventeenth Amendment: *I am the Seventeenth Amendment. I have brothers and sisters in the United States Constitution, and this is the story of my life and how I came to be.*

- Sugar Act of 1764: *I am the Sugar Act of 1764 and, boy, have I got a story to tell.*

- Australia: *I am the continent of Australia, but some might know me as a country.*

- Statue of Liberty: *I am the Statue of Liberty, and I proudly stand on a small island in Upper New York Bay.*

- Supply and demand: *My name is Supply. You probably know my friend Demand.*

Imagined conversation stories: Although not technically a story, students can create imagined conversations between historical figures of the past and the present. This style of narratives will typically be written as a dialogue with the use of quotation marks.

Sample Imagined conversation Stories

- Thomas Jefferson and Barack Obama: *"You know Tom, I have been thinking about shipping and trade interests during your time,"* Barack began slowly.

- Martin Luther King, Jr. and Gandhi: *"I always found your tactic of nonviolence fascinating,"* Dr. King mentioned.

- Abraham Lincoln and Nelson Mandela: *"I must say, Abe, I thought about you a lot in my own fight against apartheid in South Africa,"* Nelson admitted.

- Neil Armstrong and Wilbur and Orville Wright: *"Could you two have ever imagined that less than seventy years after discovering flight we would have a man on the moon?"* Neil said with amazement.

- Isaac Newton and Albert Einstein: *"I certainly do not think anything I did would have ever been possible without you,"* Einstein confessed.

Different perspective stories: By taking historical events and telling them from different perspectives, students internalize the context of the events. These stories should be told in first person.

Sample Different Perspective Stories

- American Indians on the arrival of the Pilgrims: *In the distance, we see the big ships coming toward us on Cape Cod.*

- A German citizen finding the 95 Theses: *I could not imagine what might draw such a crowd to the door of the church, but then I began to read the document.*

- Somebody driving a new Ford Model T: *That Henry Ford has certainly done it this time! I never dreamed about getting around this quickly.*

- Someone who attended the "I Have a Dream" speech: *We were all packed in, and I could hardly see, but it was a day I would never forget.*

- Escaping to freedom on the Underground Railroad: *My mother had said it's not a real railroad, but it is where we will be safe.*

"Life in" stories: Students can create stories about life in areas, civilizations, or geographical regions. These are to be written in third person.

Sample Life In Stories

- plains Indians

- The Enlightenment

- feudal Europe

- the American frontier

- migrant camp in California

Firsthand Reporting Stories: Students can select historical events and write news articles in third person.

Sample Firsthand Reporting Stories

- Montgomery Bus Boycott

- signing of the Declaration of Independence

- sentencing of Socrates

- building of the Coliseum

- storming of the Bastille

Descriptive

Social studies curriculum requires a deeper learning of material to truly grasp and apply concepts. Descriptive writing is well suited for social studies because it offers deep learning opportunities for students. As an example, when studying the Industrial Revolution of the 1900s, students learned these historical facts:

- Young children worked long hours in dangerous factory conditions.

- They worked for very little money since they could be paid less than an adult.

- Their smaller size allowed them to fit into the small work spaces of factories.

When asked to write descriptions of the conditions of child labor after looking at actual photographs from the era, their understanding deepened. They could understand the desperate conditions of the children; the on their young faces; and the cramped and dirty factories. In contrast to their lives, their understanding moved beyond facts to empathy.

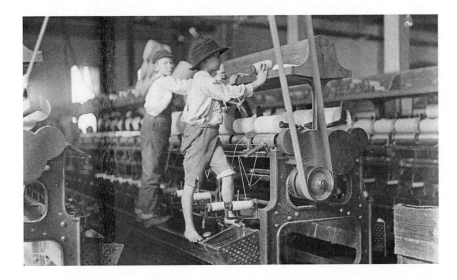

Descriptive writing depicts something in words. In social studies, many times students are writing descriptions based on visual primary sources, including paintings, photographs, and prints that show everything from landscapes to waterscapes, and from portraits to still life. Artifacts, including primary sources and replicas, are other great resources to inspire students writing descriptions. Films, including archived silent and sound films, documentaries, and modern reenactments of events in history, are sometimes not considered when prepping students for descriptive writing but are great resources.

Regardless of what is used to inspire them, students need to be given writing prompts, such as the following:

- Describe the person, people, or the object in a painting, print, or photograph.
- Describe the historical setting or background in a painting, print, or photograph.
- Describe the details of an artifact.
- Describe the activity or event depicted in a film.

Using Senses

The strength of a descriptive writing piece will always be its language—descriptive words and imagery. Underscoring these words is the use of the senses—sight, sound, taste, touch, smell, and feeling. "You can almost feel the grime caked on their faces and the exhaustion behind their eyes," as opposed to "they look dirty and tired." To help students generate the words and images that use senses in their descriptions, I have them use *Descriptive Writing* activity sheets (Figure 3.17; reproducible on page 165) as a prewriting activity.

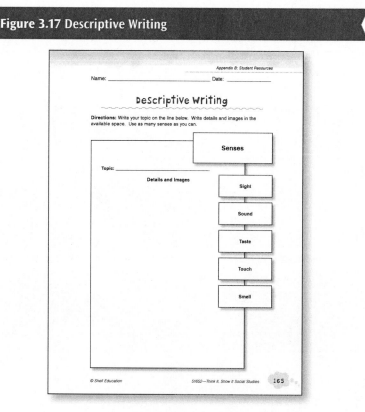

Figure 3.17 Descriptive Writing

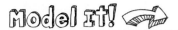 **Model It!**

> **Traveling on the *Niña, Pinta,* and *Santa María***
> (*show students prints or paintings*)
>
> - **sight:** dark and gloomy night
>
> - **sounds:** waves slapping against the ship, howl of the storm's wind and rain, sails flapping in the wind
>
> - **taste:** taste of salt water spraying over the ships
>
> - **touch:** motion of the ships tossed back and forth
>
> - **smell:** salt water in the air

Before viewing a visual primary or secondary document, start by activating students' prior knowledge about the topic. Typical questions to accomplish this for various primary sources are:

Painting, Photographs, and Prints

- What historical event is happening? What do we know about the event?

- What do we know about this person? What is his or her role in history?

- What do we know about the dress and customs of people at this historical time?

- Where is this picture's location? What do we know about its historical significance?

Artifacts

- What people or culture used this artifact?

- What materials were used in making this artifact?

- Why is this artifact important? Does it have any functional or symbolic meaning?

- What does it tell us about the place and era in which it was made?

Films, Videos, and DVDs

- What is being depicted in the film?

- What time and place is the film about?

- Do we know anything about the person or people in the film?

- What do we know about the significance of the person, time, or event presented in the film?

While studying a painting, a photograph, or a print, observing and/or touching an artifact, or watching a film, students can fill out the *Descriptive Writing* activity sheet. On the sheet, they list words, details, and images that come to mind.

For example, while studying the California Gold Rush, students were given primary source documents: an illustration of gold miners and a number of black and white photographs of gold miners. Before starting their descriptive observations, they were prompted with discussion questions for what they knew about the Gold Rush and the forty-niners.

- When and where was gold first discovered in California?
- Where did the prospective gold miners, the migrants, come from?
- How did they travel to San Francisco? What were their journeys like?
- What were the conditions of their homes and the mining camps?

Then, using the pictures, their assignment was to write descriptions of the gold miners.

From the pictures, they generated words, details, and images. These words and images became the language used in their descriptions. Some examples include these:

- black leather boots
- rolled up cotton shirts
- kneeling down
- sunbaked faces

- sweaty
- tattered, ragged clothes
- up to their knees in water, mud, and dirt
- wide-brimmed hats

Descriptive and Precise Words

Coinciding with the words, details, and images gathered with the *Descriptive Writing* activity sheet is the skill of selecting more descriptive and precise word choices. Rather than saying "they wore boots," a more descriptive and precise detail is that "they wore knee-high, black leather boots." Rather than writing that the forty-niners had hats, a more detailed observation is that they wore "wide-brimmed hats."

Begin this classroom activity by passing out a series of pictures of people, places, or things. Each student gets one picture, and all students are to write two-sentence descriptions of the people, places, or things in their pictures. Explain to students, "You can write only two sentences, so you have to rely on precise words." Then, spread the pictures on a table, and have students read their "two-sentence descriptions" while the rest of the class tries to guess which picture is being described. Included here are two example pictures with sample student descriptions:

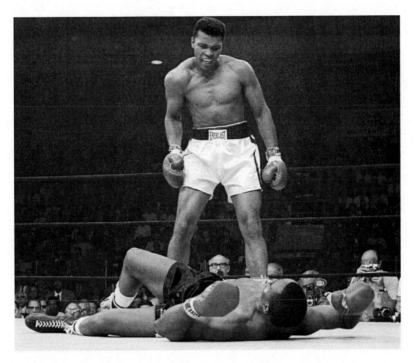

Muscles tight, granted like the branches of an old cypress tree. His brow furrowed, and eyes daring his opponent to get back up.

Unshowered, unshaven, hungry, tired, and lonesome even though they are in a crowd. Their slumping posture and timeworn hats portray a life of hard times.

Word webs can also be very helpful for both beginning and advanced students. Encourage students to create word webs using thesauruses or dictionaries. This is done in an effort to help them develop the habit of selecting the best synonyms for their descriptions.

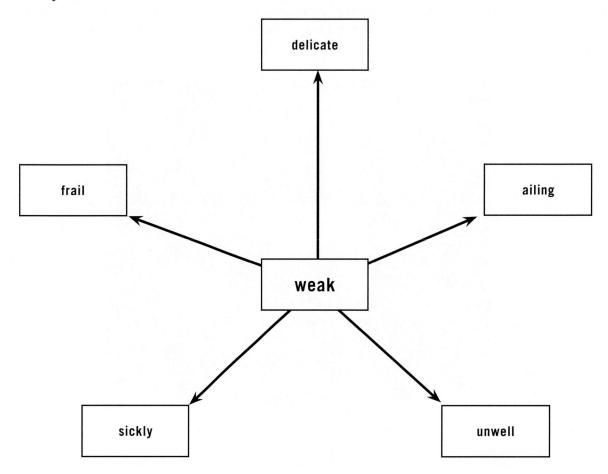

While the writings that have been outlined in this section have been single-purpose writing tasks (i.e., to describe), longer written pieces (i.e., persuasive, arguments, and/or explanatory) often integrate descriptive sections or passages. Reports and essays frequently need to include descriptions as well as comparisons and explanations of causes and effects.

Cause and Effect

Analyzing cause and effect is a critical part of inquiries done in social studies. It addresses the question: *What are the causal relationships between or among events, conditions, or behaviors?* Students begin to write about causes and effects, first by determining the different causes. Then, they must find the effects.

- To determine the cause, students should ask themselves: *Why did this happen, or what were the causes? What are the factors that caused this?*

- To determine effects, students should ask themselves: *What happened because of this? What is the effect or result? What are the factors that resulted from this cause?*

Using the *Cause and Effect* activity sheet (Figure 3.18; reproducible on page 166) students can answer questions in relation to topics, such as the stock market crash of 1929.

Figure 3.18 Cause and Effect

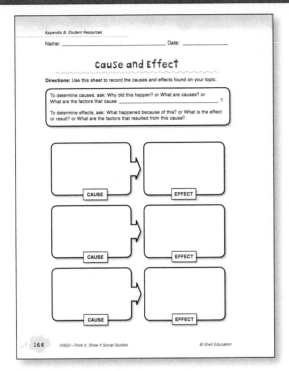

Blank Reproducible

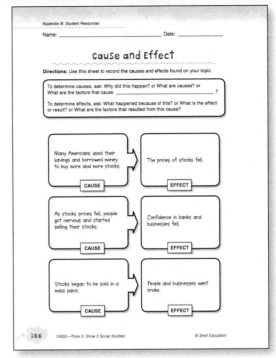

Student Example

The example presented above shows that students determined three different causes and effects for the stock market crash. This demonstrates what is called a "chain of causes and effects." This is where one event (cause) precipitates another event (effect), which triggers another event, and so on and so forth. The result is a chain of successive events.

Having assembled the causes and effects, students can practice writing cause-and-effect sentences using the *Cause-and-Effect Sentences* activity sheet (Figure 3.19 on page 82; reproducible on page 167). First, each student writes a cause and effect in the rounded rectangles at the top of the sheet. Then, he or she writes a "cause-first sentence" (1) where the sentence starts with the cause and is followed by its effect (subordinate clause). Next, each student draws a box around one or more of the cause-and-effect words shown at the bottom of the sheet:

- **Because** people began to use their savings and borrow money to buy stocks, more and more stocks were sold, and **consequently**, prices began to fall.

Next, write an "effect-first sentence" (2) in the same way as the "cause-first sentence" except the effect will begin the sentence.

- The price of stocks dropped **as a result of** people using their savings and borrowing money to buy more and more stocks.

Figure 3.19 Cause-and-Effect Sentences

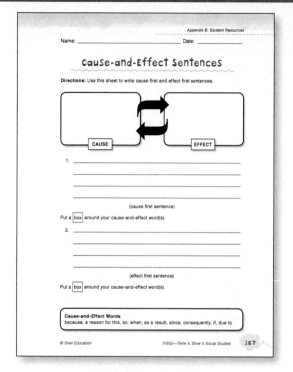

Blank Reproducible

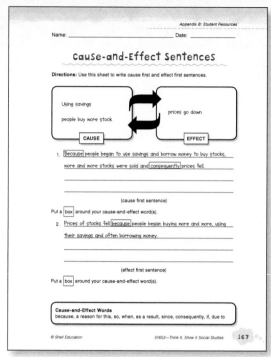

Student Example

There are three additional models for cause and effects: single cause and effects, multiple effects, and multiple causes.

- A **single cause and effect** is simply where a cause leads to a single effect/event. For example: *As a result of the invention of the sextant, early explorers were able to navigate the oceans and seas by measuring the positions of the stars and sun.*

- **Multiple effects** are where one cause leads to more than one effect/event. For example: *When a person texts while driving, many dangerous things happen. First, texting takes the driver's mind off the task of driving. Secondly, texting requires the driver's hands, eyes, and brain to work at the same time.*

- **Multiple causes** are where more than one cause leads to one effect/event. For example: *The overwhelming victory of the Confederate at First Battle of Bull Run was due to two important factors. First, there was a five-day delay after the Union Army moved toward Manassas Junction before the fighting actually began. Consequently, this gave time for Confederate reinforcements to arrive just as the North was winning the battle. The second factor was the heroic stand made by General Thomas A. Jackson, who became known as Stonewall Jackson.*

Another activity for more advanced students is called cause-and–effect mapping. You can use this activity when breaking down more complex readings with more content. Have students read articles and map out the causes and effects.

The *Cause-and-Effect Mapping* sheet (Figure 3.20; reproducible on page 168) is an effective tool for students. The student example below was created after reading an article on the fall of the Roman Empire.

Figure 3.20 Cause-and-Effect Mapping

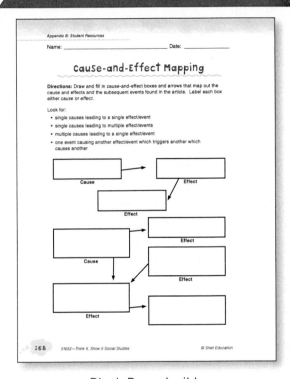

Blank Reproducible   Student Example

Topics and Prompt Questions

The following topics and prompt questions are strong examples to encourage rigorous classroom discussions. Use these examples to write further questions for the social studies topics you teach in your classroom.

Government and Civics: Citizenship

Compare and Contrast What's the difference between being a good citizen and being a bad citizen?	**Opinion** In your opinion, what are the most important responsibilities a citizen has to his or her community?
Explanatory/Informative Choose a historical figure and explain what made him or her a good citizen.	**Narrative** Tell about a time when you demonstrated or witnessed good citizenship.
Descriptive If someone were new to the country, how would you describe what it means to be a good citizen?	**Cause and Effect** Describe how a historical figure was able to make a difference by demonstrating good citizenship.

Geography: Human Environment Interaction

Compare and Contrast How do humans affect the environment? Pick an area or region, and explain what it was like before people inhabited it and what it is like today.	**Opinion** In your opinion, has the environment been helped or harmed by humans?
Explanatory/Informative Explain what human environment is, and provide three examples of how people and nature shape each other.	**Narrative** Write a story about a time when you or your family did something outdoors together, such as gardening, hiking, or going to the beach.
Descriptive Describe your favorite outdoor activity, such as playing in a park or going for a hike. What do you see, feel, hear, and smell when you do this activity?	**Cause and Effect** Describe how humans change and affect the environment to meet their needs. Or explain how humans have adapted their lifestyles to the environment.

History: Founding Fathers

Compare and Contrast Pick two Founding Fathers, and compare their lives. Where were they from? What did they accomplish? Why are they important to U.S. history?	**Opinion** In your opinion, which Founding Father had the greatest impact on the young nation?
Explanatory/Informative Give a brief biography of one Founding Father that provides the reader with information about his life.	**Narrative** Tell a story about one of the Founding Fathers that reflects his beliefs or leadership.
Descriptive Describe one of the Founding Fathers. What was his physical appearance like? What did he like to do?	**Cause and Effect** Write about what motivated the Founding Fathers to act on their beliefs and how things changed as a result of their actions.

Geography: Regions

Compare and Contrast Compare and contrast two regions of the United States. What is similar and different about these two areas?	**Opinion** Pick one region of the United States, and convince the reader why it is the most important or best region in the country.
Explanatory/Informative Explain what makes one region distinct. What unites places within this region? What makes it unique or different from neighboring regions?	**Narrative** Write about a time when you visited or had guests visiting from another region. What do you think their experience was like being in a different environment?
Descriptive Describe what it might be like to live in one of the regions within the United States. What is the weather like on a day-to-day basis? What do people do for fun there?	**Cause and Effect** Describe how one region has changed over time. What was the region like fifty years ago, and what is it like today? What caused this change to occur?

History: Civil War

Compare and Contrast Compare and contrast the Union and the Confederacy. Who were the leaders of each group? What were the goals for each? What advantages and disadvantages did each side have?	**Opinion and Argument** Choose one of the following, and provide two or three reasons why it was a cause of the Civil War: • slavery • states' rights • social and economic differences
Explanatory/Informative Explain why the South seceded from the Union.	**Narrative** Tell a story about an event from the Civil War from the perspective of a soldier, nurse, or citizen of either the North or the South.
Descriptive Choose a photograph of the Civil War, and write a vivid description of its scene.	**Cause and Effect** How did differences in beliefs, values, and lifestyles create divisions that led to the Civil War?

Economics: Supply and Demand

Compare and Contrast What is the difference between supply and demand? Which people/groups supply products? Which people/groups demand products?	**Opinion and Argument** In your opinion, who should be in charge of managing and regulating markets? Should it be entirely up to companies? The government? A mixture of the two?
Explanatory/Informative Explain why a lot of companies sell similar products (for example, shoes). What is the benefit of giving consumers choices and variety?	**Narrative** Write about a time when you went to a store, market, or auction. What types of products were supplied, and what type of people demanded them?
Descriptive Describe how a resource becomes a product to be sold at a market.	**Cause and Effect** How does a change in demand for a product affect the price and supply of that product?

Summaries

The authors of *Classroom Instruction that Works: Research-Based Strategies for Increasing Student Achievement*, Robert Marzano, Debra Pickering, and Jane Pollock (2001), explain that, when writing a summary, students need to be engaged in three activities (30):

- **Deleting some information**—Is there information that is unnecessary to the overall meaning of the passage?

- **Substituting some information**—Can I substitute a more general word or idea that would cover some of the ideas or details in the passage without having to write it out?

- **Keeping some information**—What information is central to the overall meaning of the passage? What supporting details are necessary for understanding the information?

The authors say that these activities "demand a fair amount of analysis of the information being summarized" (31). When students summarize what they are reading, they must be able to identify a main idea, differentiate between the most important information and the less critical, and condense this into succinct and coherent texts. "Summarizing is one of the most powerful skills students can cultivate. It provides students with tools for identifying the most important aspects of what they are learning" (48).

Student Strategies

Key Words

A strategy developed by Jeff Hoyt (1999) called Key Words is where beginning students are given short passages. With the passages, students identify and share what they think are its key words. After a discussion of the passage and its key words, students write short summaries using some of those key words. When using this strategy, have students identify both key words and key phrases.

The next page describes an example of how to apply this strategy in your classroom.

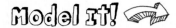 **Model It!**

> ### Passage: Patrick Henry
>
> Patrick Henry spoke to his fellow Virginians, urging them to take up arms in self-defense. Great Britain had gone too far in imposing taxes on Americans, and it was time for the colonists to defend themselves. He ended his speech with the words "I know not what course others may take; but as for me, give me liberty or give me death."
>
> ### Key Words and Phrases
>
> self-defense, take up arms, imposing taxes, defend, speech, colonists, liberty, Great Britain
>
> ### Summary: Patrick Henry
>
> Henry said to take up arms and defend themselves because England was imposing taxes on the colonists.

Guided Instruction with Summaries

When building on experiences, such as seeking out key words and phrases, all students benefit from guided instruction. This strategy can be adjusted to increase or decrease rigor to better match individual students' ability levels. With this process, you can lead students through passages by modeling and with explicit instruction. Address these questions and tasks:

Guided Summary Questions/Tasks

What is the topic?

- Circle the word or words of the topic.

What is the topic sentence?

- Underline the topic sentence.

What is the main idea?

- What key words are found in the topic sentence and main idea? Put checks over the key words found in the topic sentence and the main idea.
- Using the key words, write a complete sentence about the main idea.

What are the important point(s) about the main idea?

- List, as phrases, the important point(s) about the main idea.
- Put checks over any additional key words you find.
- Write out the phrase(s) as a complete sentence(s).

Here is a passage adapted from Stewart and Polly Anne Graff's book, *Helen Keller: Crusader for the Blind and Deaf.*

Helen Keller couldn't hear, see, and did not speak. She lived in a dark and lonely world until Annie Sullivan came to teach her. Annie traced letters and words in Helen's hand, and made Helen realize she could "talk" to people. Eager to make up for lost time, Helen threw herself into her studies. She decided to teach others about the special training blind and deaf children need. Helen traveled across the globe and raised money to start up schools for deaf and blind children.

Guided Summary Questions for Helen Keller

What is the topic?

- Helen Keller

What is the topic sentence?

- "Helen Keller couldn't hear, see, and did not speak."

What is the main idea?

- "Annie Sullivan taught Helen to 'talk' to people."

What are key words found in both the topic sentence and main idea?

- Put checks over the key words found in the topic sentence and main idea: "taught" and "'talk' to people"

Using the key words, write a complete sentence about the main idea.

- "Helen Keller was taught to 'talk' to people."

What are the important points about the main idea?

- "traced letters" and "words in Helen's hand"; "taught others about special training"

Put checks over any additional key words you find.

- "traced," "special training," "deaf," and "blind"

Write out the phrase(s) as a complete sentence(s).

- "Annie taught her by tracing letters and words in her hand." "Helen taught others about the special training for deaf and blind children."

Guiding students with these questions, first ask them to comprehend the piece: What is the topic? Topic sentence? Main idea? Important points? Then, by writing the main idea with their key words, they have one of the sentences for their summaries. By listing in phrases the important points about their main ideas, they have kept some information and deleted some information (the information that they didn't list as important points). Finally, by writing out the phrases in complete sentences, they have the sentences for completing their summaries. Here is an example:

Helen Keller

Helen Keller could not speak, hear, or talk. She learned to "talk" to people when Annie Sullivan taught her by tracing letters and words in her hands. Helen taught others about the special training for deaf and blind children.

As students mature, many of the same challenges they had as younger students remain. Their texts may be longer and more complex, but they still need to analyze the texts to be able to state main ideas, locate major points, and differentiate between critical information with supporting details and less important information. Students still need to be able to present this in concise summaries.

The *Summary/Information Web* (Figure 4.1; reproducible on page 169) is what students fill out to refer to when they write their summaries. In the circle on the left, they write the topic of the passage with its main idea. Then, using the circles on the right, they fill in the important information and any necessary details to understand the information. They also indicate the source of what they are summarizing. Note that while the sheet has only three information circles, some passages that more advanced students need to summarize will often have more than three areas to address. Advanced students should be informed to simply add unlined paper to their sheets and draw the additional circles if needed.

In one instance, students were provided with the following passage from an article about Sputnik. In addition to the passage, students watched a video presentation on the space race between the United States and the Soviet Union. Students then completed the *Summary/Information Web* sheets. Figure 4.1 includes an example student response.

Sputnik

After World War II, the United States' mistrust of the Soviet Union grew due to the Soviet Union's military expansion into Eastern Europe. Also, they had now exploded an atomic bomb. In 1957, they launched the first satellite called Sputnik. It was polished steel, so it would reflect light that could be seen around the world. It broadcast a "beep-beep" signal that could be picked up by radio operators. The United States reacted with fear. There was a satellite flying over the top of the United States. They wondered if the Russians had rockets powerful enough to launch a satellite. Did they have rockets powerful enough to launch atomic bombs on America? The space race had begun.

Figure 4.1 Summary/Information Web

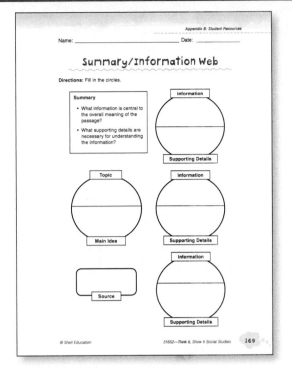

Blank Reproducible

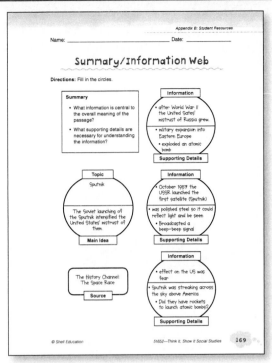

Student Example

Graphs

Some information students encounter in social studies texts and articles may be presented visually with graphs. Students may be asked to summarize their interpretations of graphs outright or to integrate the information or data attained from a graph within the larger summary of a text.

Bar, circle, and line graphs are important parts of how social scientists communicate information. Graphs allow a lot of data to be condensed into single, visual forms. Students studying population growth with the chart below, for example, are provided with a great deal of information. The graph includes the size of the world's population in the years 1850, 1900, 1950, 1990, and 2000. Between what years was the greatest population growth? The slowest?

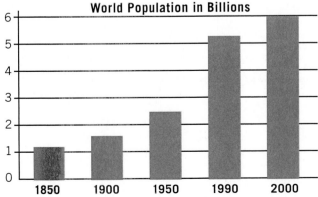

Single Graph Summaries

Learning to interpret a graph and write a summary of it goes hand-in-hand. One reinforces the other. In an examination of a graph, ask students a question about information gleaned from the graph. When students answer, ask a follow-up question: "How do we know that?" A single graph summary does the same thing by asking, *What do I know?* and *How do I know it?*

Beginning students can write graph summary statements to show their interpretive understandings of a graph. The *What Do I Know* is their "data interpretation" and the *How Do I Know It* becomes evidence statements. With the graph below (Figure 4.2), students can use the *Writing Graph Summary Statements* activity sheet (Figure 4.3; reproducible on page 170) to summarize the information on the graph. Figure 4.3 includes a student example based on this graph for your reference.

Figure 4.2 How Much Water Do Homes Use?

How Much Water do Homes Use?

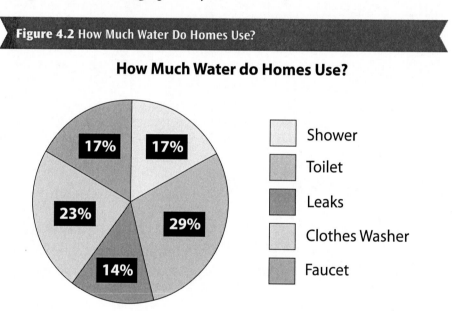

Students can now interpret the circle graph. It shows that the largest percentage of water used in homes is in our toilets. Students know this because 29 percent of our water is used in our toilets, whereas all the other uses are less than 29 percent. In addition, the graph tells students that leaks cause the least water to be used. Students know this because it has only 14 percent while the rest are all higher.

Figure 4.3 Writing Graph Summary Statements

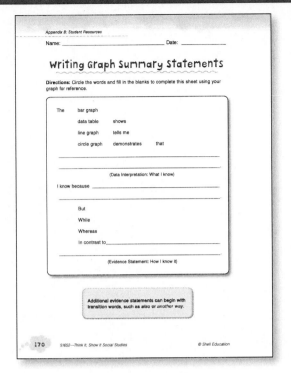

Blank Reproducible

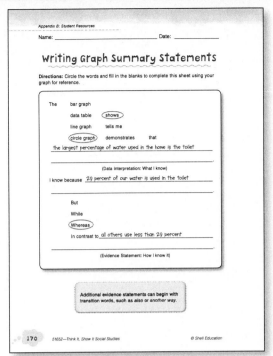

Student Example

Language of Graphs

More advanced students who understand how to interpret the information presented in graphs will many times need to incorporate that data into their summaries. Here, they need to know the language of graphs. These are the words and phrases used to describe what information a graph shows. Using the pattern shown in the *Graph Sentences* sheet (Figure 4.4; reproducible on page 171), they can easily do so. Figure 4.4 includes a student example for your reference.

Figure 4.4 Graph Sentences

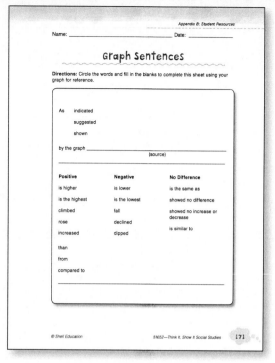

Blank Reproducible

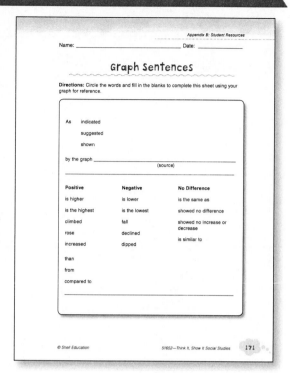

Student Example

The following is an example of a student summary of the Workforce–Participation Rate Graph (Figure 4.5).

As indicated by the graph, the workforce participation in the United States grew between 1970 and 2000. It reached the highest in 2000 with 67.5 percent participation compared to 60 percent in 1970. After 2000 the participation declined by 5 percent to 62.5 percent in 2013.

Figure 4.5 Workforce-Participation Rate Graph

Workforce-Participation Rate
(seasonally adjusted)

Academic Vocabulary

Car, school, run, and *happy.* These are frequently encountered words that continually circulate around students and are thereby learned indirectly through daily interactions with oral and written language. High frequency, but more abstract words, such as *antique, ridiculous,* and *anticipate,* are more challenging. Focused instruction with words such as these should be a part of reading comprehension strategies. Anderson and Freebody's research has clearly documented that vocabulary is related to and affects comprehension (1981, 77–117). The combination of frequently encountered and high frequency words are the wellspring of students' vocabulary both in and out of school.

There are words less informally encountered (if at all) in the life of the average student. These words can be broken down into two classes. **General academic vocabulary** is what many educators call words used across content areas with academic reading, writing, and speaking. *Analogy, analyze, contradict, distinguish, equivalent,* and *irrelevant* are examples of words used throughout the different academic content areas. The other category of words is called **domain-specific words** and is described as words that are specific to a domain or field of study. For example, domain-specific words such as *boundary, census, climate, cultivation, ecology,* and *economy* are critical to the study of geography in the intermediate grades. These are considered domain specific because they are words found within the learning domain of geography. Oftentimes these words cannot be determined via context clues, but rather require a dictionary.

Both categories of words are part of academic language. Along with individual vocabulary words, academic language encompasses the forms, phrases, and sentence structures used in academic writing. It is the type of writing social studies students encounter in informational texts, supplementary articles, and reference materials. Looking back at the *Compare-and-Contrast Sentences* activity sheet that was introduced in Chapter 2 (Figure 2.9 on page 33), notice the language of these sentences with the comparison of latitude and longitude. The general academic vocabulary is italicized`, while the domain-specific words are in bold.

- Both the **latitude** and the **longitude** help us *determine* the **absolute** location of a place on a **global grid**.

- **Latitude** *measures* the north and south *boundaries* from the **equator** in contrast to the **longitude**, which *measures* the east and west *boundaries* from the **prime meridian**.

- **Longitude** is *referred* to in **degrees** (i.e., 90°) in the same way as **latitude**.

- Lines of the **latitude** are called **parallels** because they are **parallel** to each other. On the other hand, lines of the **longitude** are called **meridians**, and they meet at the North and South Poles.

- **Latitude numbers** are *located* on the sides of maps unlike **longitude numbers** which are *located* on the tops of **maps**.

Explicit instruction with academic language is essential in social studies classrooms if it is to become a working part of students' writing. Domain-specific vocabulary in social studies is firmly moored to its topic's content. In other words, students need the vocabulary to understand the content, and they need the content to give context to the vocabulary. For example, to understand who the abolitionists were, students need an understanding of slaves and the institution of slavery, slave and free states, southern cotton industry, and emancipation. Collecting or bringing together words associated with a topic is a strategy that connects vocabulary with its content.

Concept Word Walls

Word walls in social studies classrooms can be very helpful for students to acquire vocabulary. A word wall displays domain-specific words (sometimes with their meanings and illustrations) on a wall. These words are collected from what students are hearing, reading, discussing, viewing, or investigating. For example, students studying the Lewis and Clark Expedition collected these words:

- continent
- expedition
- explore
- journaling
- keelboats
- Louisiana Territory
- maps

- mountain pass
- navigate
- pirogues
- river rapids
- supplies
- surveying
- villages

Groupings

From the word wall of the Lewis and Clark Expedition, students sorted the words into different groups showing what they have in common. Oftentimes, terms can be grouped into multiple categories. Regardless of how students choose to group, they need to be able to verbalize their reasoning as to why they grouped the words as they did.

- **Land areas:** continent, Louisiana Territory
- **Means of travel:** keelboats, pirogues
- **Activities:** explore, navigate, surveying, journaling
- **Materials:** supplies, maps, journals
- **Geographical features:** mountain passes, river rapids, villages
- **Common Suffixes:** surveying, journaling, passes, rapids, villages, maps, supplies, journals, keelboats, pirogues
- **Built from root words:** explore, exploration, expedition, navigate, navigation
- **Synonyms:** expedition/trip, explore/tour, navigate/guide, pass/gorge

Connection Sentences

Another vocabulary strategy for students is to write connection sentences. Here, students show how different words are connected directly within the context of what they are studying. They model their sentences from two connection sentence patterns. One pattern is used when students are connecting only two words. Another is when they are connecting three words.

---

connecting two words

Topic _____

_____ (word) is connected to _____ (word) because _____ (reason).

---

connecting three words

Topic _____

_____ (word) is connected to _____ (word) and _____ (word)

because _____ (reason).

The *Connection Sentences* sheet (Figure 5.1; reproducible on page 172) helps students with writing these types of sentences. The student example below is from a study of the Civil Rights Movement.

Figure 5.1 Connection Sentences

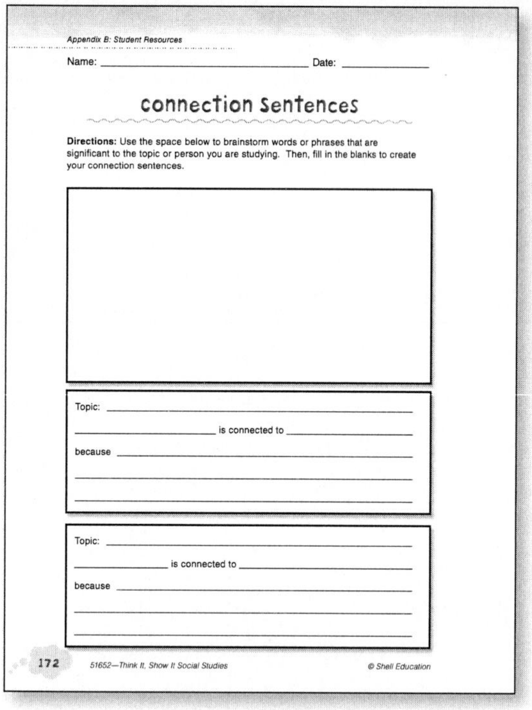
Appendix B: Student Resources

Name: ______________ Date: ______

connection sentences

Directions: Use the space below to brainstorm words or phrases that are significant to the topic or person you are studying. Then, fill in the blanks to create your connection sentences.

Topic: ______________

______ is connected to ______

because ______________

Topic: ______________

______ is connected to ______

because ______________

172 51652—Think It, Show It Social Studies © Shell Education

Blank Reproducible

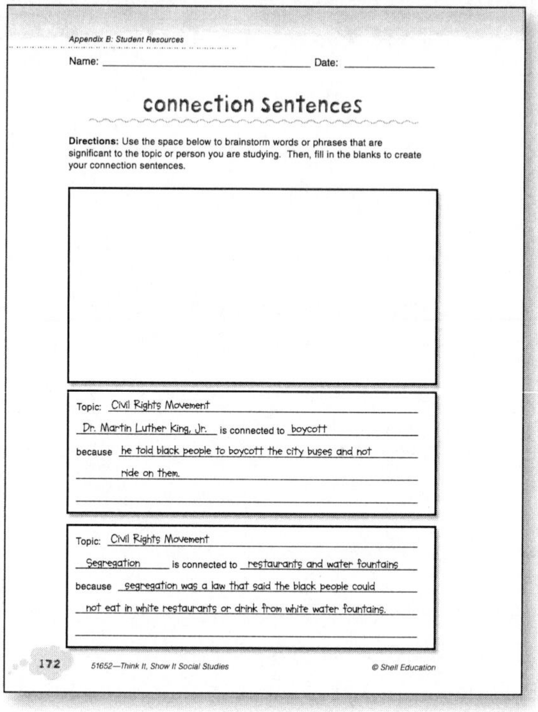
Appendix B: Student Resources

Name: ______________ Date: ______

connection sentences

Directions: Use the space below to brainstorm words or phrases that are significant to the topic or person you are studying. Then, fill in the blanks to create your connection sentences.

Topic: Civil Rights Movement

Dr. Martin Luther King, Jr. is connected to boycott

because he told black people to boycott the city buses and not ride on them.

Topic: Civil Rights Movement

Segregation is connected to restaurants and water fountains

because segregation was a law that said the black people could not eat in white restaurants or drink from white water fountains.

172 51652—Think It, Show It Social Studies © Shell Education

Student Example

Used together, word walls, grouping words, and connection sentences are great strategies to help students learn and obtain both domain-specific and general academic vocabulary.

Pre-Reading Strategies

Pre-reading strategies can support better comprehension and understanding of critical vocabulary, textbook chapters, supplementary articles, videos and films, and classroom presentations. These strategies are the foundation of instruction in social studies, as they contain the content students need to learn. As students read or listen to these, they encounter new, unfamiliar vocabulary. Many textbooks have highlighted key words that are explained in definition sidebars or glossaries. Along with easily accessible definitions, textbooks often are deliberately written to provide students with support in determining the meaning of key words. (e.g., As these groups became less nomadic, they stopped moving from place to place and settled in river valleys and near lakes.) Following are two suggestions with accompanying examples.

Matching Vocabulary

Before reading a passage, article, or book, give students a *Vocabulary Pre-Test* (Figure 5.2; reproducible on page 173). The first contains a list of key words from the selection. Across from it is another column with short meanings for each term. Students draw lines from one column to the other, matching the words with their meanings. After reading the text, students are to locate the exact sentences that confirm their matches. Figure 5.2 includes an example using *George Washington Carver: Planting Ideas* by Jennifer Kroll.

Figure 5.2 Vocabulary Pre-Test

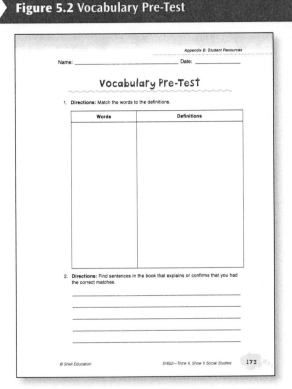

Blank Reproducible   Student Example

Vocabulary Assessment

A similar strategy involves the *Pre-Reading Vocabulary Assessment* (Figure 5.3 on page 100; reproducible on page 175). On this sheet, there are key words from the text students will read. Students check the column based on their knowledge of the word; column (A) if they have no idea of what the word means; (B) if they have heard or seen the word, but can't really define it; (C) if they know what it means and can write a "working definition." After reading the selection, they return to the sheet and write a correct definition for each of the words. If needed, they compare their working definitions to what they learned from the text and then write accurate definitions for each of those words. For your reference, page 174 is an example vocabulary assessment based on the article, "Natural Disasters Information: Blizzard."

Figure 5.3 Pre-Reading Vocabulary Assessment

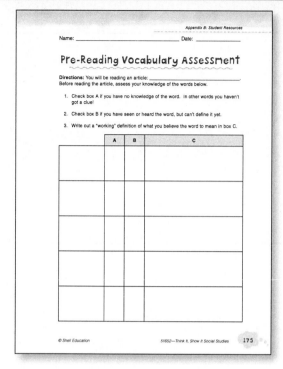

Blank Reproducible

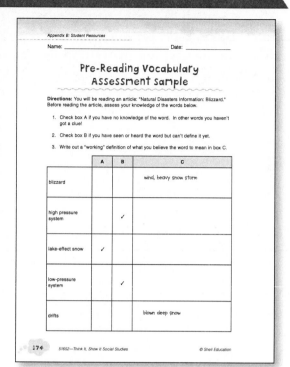

Student Example

Word Mastery: General Academic Vocabulary

Figure 2.8 (page 32) in Chapter 2 includes an example of a completed *Word Mastery* activity sheet for the words *comprised* and *enacting*. *Word Mastery* activity sheets are best used to help students with abstract and consequently more difficult words. Through pictures, artifacts, and digital media, students studying Southwest Indians, for example, easily come to understand concrete words, such as *wickiups, maize, kiva,* and *pueblo*. General academic vocabulary words, such as *originally, acquired, influence,* and *distinctive,* from that same unit of study require deeper analysis.

Using this sheet, students look up the words they are learning and fill in these critical areas:

1. word

2. part of speech

3. dictionary definition

4. synonym

5. antonym

6. association

7. different context

There are numerous ways this sheet can be used in the classroom:

1. Words can be assigned to individual students to be shared with the whole class.

2. Students choose their own words, fill out the sheet, and have a guessing game with the class by reading all pieces except number one.

3. Include the words on classroom Word Walls and have students use the words in "connection sentences" with other words from their unit of study.

4. A collection of the sheets can be bound into a book as a reference.

5. Sheets can be used for students to create their own dictionaries, which include pictorial representations of the words.

6. Have students write metaphors and riddles for their words.

7. Have students look for and record when they see the words in different contexts (newspapers, brochures, advertisements, etc.).

8. Have students include a word analysis of their words. For example, root form, affixes, and other words built from the root form (origin, original, originally).

9. Write the vocabulary words and definitions at the top of legal-size paper and post the papers on a wall where students can reach them. Provide a selection of pens, markers, and pencils nearby. As a class, ask students to come up to jot down examples or personal revelations regarding the words throughout the unit.

10. Set up a technology center, including access to the Internet, where students can produce and publish their *Word Mastery* activity sheets as well as interact and leave appropriate feedback for each other.

Classroom Strategies

Thinking Through Your Writing

The *Thinking Through Your Writing* activity sheet (Figure 6.1; reproducible on page 144) is designed to accomplish exactly what the title states—*Thinking Through Your Writing*. As a prewriting activity, it helps students "think through" a specific piece of writing. On the sheet, they state their topic, the purpose or type of writing they will be employing, and the format in which it will be written. In addition, they generate "questions" their writing might address.

Figure 6.1 Thinking Through Your Writing

Appendix B: Student Resources

Name: _____   Date: _____

Thinking Through Your Writing

Directions: Use this to plan your writing.

Topic: _____

_____

Purpose: _____

_____

_____

Questions My Writing Will Answer:

1. _____

2. _____

3. _____

4. _____

What Form Will My Writing Take?

_____

144   51652—Think It, Show It Social Studies   © Shell Education

Although the sheet can be used independently by students, very often the "questions my writing will answer" are generated in class. Classroom discussions center around what information is central to understanding research topics. For example, when writing reports on different countries, start the discussion with an overarching question: "What information would the reader need to best understand the country that is being written about?" Together the class discusses and compiles a list.

- What are the physical features of the country? Rivers? Mountains? Deserts? Lakes? Oceans? Seas?

- How do the country's physical features affect how people live?

- What is the country's climate?

- Are there distinctive foods? Dress? Customs?

- Is the country predominantly urban or rural?

- What are the country's major exports?

- What are the country's natural resources?

- What effect does the country's climate have on the products it produces?

- What form of government exists?

Beginning their inquiry with questions in mind helps students focus their research. The questions function as a scaffold or foundation that directs the aim of their research. Students do not just read about the country they are researching and blindly copy whatever information or facts they find. Rather, they connect their research and their final written product with the ideas and content of what they have been studying in class.

Add a Biographical Fact

Another prewriting activity along the same lines of the *Thinking Through Your Writing* activity sheet is the *Add a Biographical Fact* activity sheet (Figure 6.2; reproducible on page 145). Again, students identify their topic and questions to consider. On the sheet, they write a bulleted list of the information they find during their research. When appropriate, have students include a citation for each of the bulleted items indicating their text evidence. Also, to help them with the initial organization of their text, have them write a number next to each of their bulleted pieces of information suggesting their probable sequence.

Figure 6.2 Add a Biographical Fact Planning Sheet

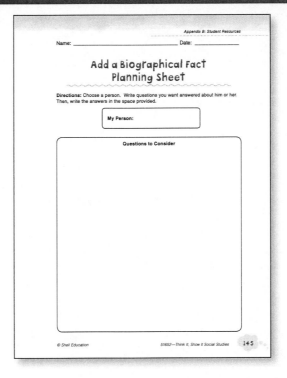

Using the filled-in sheet, students write a biographical fact poem. This format is where students add one biographical fact to each successive, repeating line. The poems are then presented as a guessing game to the class.

Who Am I?

A

A scientist

A scientist born in 1867

A scientist born in 1867, the first woman to win a Nobel Prize

A scientist born in 1867, the first woman to win a Nobel Prize whose work with her husband led to the discovery of polonium

A scientist born in 1867, the first woman to win a Nobel Prize whose work with her husband led to the discovery of polonium and later the development of X-rays.

(Who Am I?—*Marie Curie*)

This repetitive pattern can also be used creatively with a multitude of topics and content. Here, for example, is a poem written by a fifth grader while studying states.

Nebraska

Beautiful Nebraska

Beautiful, corn-growing Nebraska

Beautiful, corn-growing, cattle-grazing Nebraska

Beautiful, corn-growing, cattle-grazing, pheasant-hunting Nebraska

Beautiful, corn-growing, cattle-grazing, pheasant-hunting, North Platte river-running Nebraska

Beautiful, corn-growing, cattle-grazing, pheasant-hunting, North Platte river-running, where my grandmother lives Nebraska.

Nebraska.

Getting started with writing poems such as these, students use the *Adding Facts Planning Sheet* (Figure 6.3; reproducible on page 146).

Figure 6.3 Adding Facts Planning Sheet

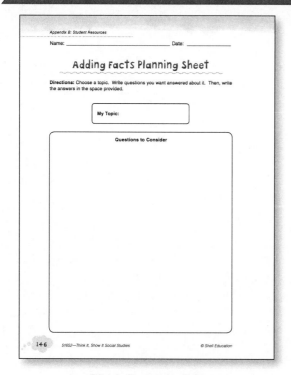

Blank Reproducible

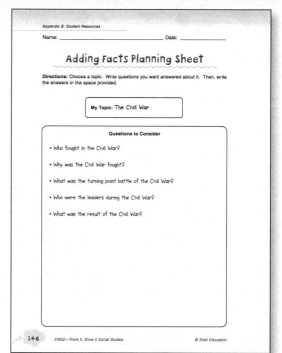

Student Example

Having identified the topics you want your students to write about, you can have them fill out these planning sheets independently or have a collaborative discussion where the class generates critical "questions to consider." Below are examples of possible topics for both the *Add a Biographical Fact Sheet* and the *Adding Facts Planning Sheet*.

Historical American Women

- Martha Washington
- Harriet Tubman
- Susan B. Anthony
- Elizabeth Cady Stanton
- Rosa Parks

Modern American Presidents

- John F. Kennedy
- Jimmy Carter
- Ronald Reagan
- George Bush
- Bill Clinton
- Barack Obama
- Donald Trump

World History Figures

- Hammurabi
- Napoleon Bonaparte
- Alexander the Great
- Julius Caesar

U.S. Constitutional Amendments and Their Effects

- Thirteenth Amendment: Abolition of Slavery
- Fourteenth Amendment: Due Process of Law
- Eighteenth Amendment: Prohibition
- Nineteenth Amendment: Women's Suffrage
- Twenty-First Amendment: Repeal of Prohibition
- Twenty-Sixth Amendment: Voting Age (18)

American Indian Tribes

- Cherokee
- Pawnee
- Arapaho
- Iroquois
- Dakota

Themes of Geography

- unique characteristics about a place
- shared characteristics of a region
- the interaction of humans and the environment
- the movement and transfer of people, ideas, and goods
- numeric vs. descriptive aspects of relative and absolute location

Venn Diagram

A *Venn Diagram* (Figure 6.4; reproducibles on page 176) is commonly used as an "assembling content" strategy. At the top of the sheet, students write the topic of their comparison. Then, to the sides of each circle, they write the subjects. In the outer circles, students record information or facts that are unique to their subjects. Where the circles overlap, they record information or facts that are shared by the two subjects.

It is important to mention that although Venn diagrams are generally filled with words and phrases, they can easily be pictorial. For example, younger students can draw and paste in the circles the different artifacts used by the colonists and native tribes. Photographs or illustrations of historical figures can be included on the diagram with their comparisons. By using Venn diagrams, students not only assemble content for their writing, but they also analyze ideas and concepts to help describe them in their own words. Venn diagrams help students activate their prior knowledge and visually structure what they are learning. The diagrams support students in selecting and organizing what they will be writing.

An extension of the standard Venn diagram, where only two concepts or ideas are being compared, is the *Triple Venn Diagram* (Figure 6.4; reproducible on page 177). With this graphic organizer, students compare and contrast three concepts. On it, students record the shared and unique characteristics between their three concepts.

Figure 6.4 Venn Diagram and Triple Venn Diagram

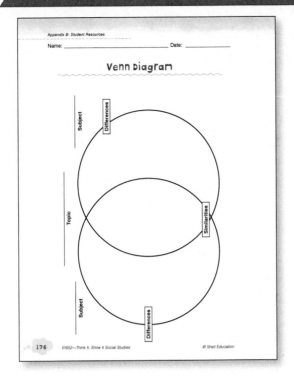

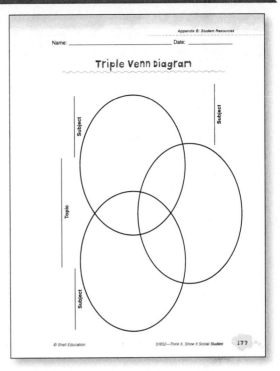

They can be used to compare and contrast an endless number of social studies concepts and ideas, such as:

- artifacts used by colonists and American Indians
- historical figures: Lincoln and Washington
- maps and globes
- differences and similarities between states of the Union
- differences and similarities between state and federal government
- life in a different time period contrasted with now
- life in different historical time periods
- features of the North and South before the Civil War

They can also be used to personalize what students are learning:

- What are the shared attributes between you and Martin Luther King Jr.? What attributes did King have that you do not? What attributes do you have that King did not?
- What characteristics are common between a colonial family and your family? What are differences?
- What are the geographical differences between where you live and that of a different area of the world? What are their similarities?

By using the Triple Venn diagram, students gain a deeper understanding of the interconnectedness of concepts:

- What characteristics are unique to the three individual subjects?

- What characteristics are shared between all three subjects?

- What characteristics are shared between pairs of subjects?

Triple Venn diagrams are particularly beneficial when advanced students are examining broader, more complex topics. For example, teachers might want to use more than one Triple Venn diagram when comparing different civilizations by examining the differences and similarities between:

- economics

- geographies

- religions

- social structures

- weather

Here is a sampling of three-concept comparisons with "cue questions" for students to consider:

Greek Philosophers: Socrates, Plato, and Aristotle

- What did each believe in?

- How did they record their ideas?

- How did they encourage others to think?

Mesoamerican Indigenous Groups: Mayas, Aztecs, and Incas

- Where was each group geographically located?

- How long was each group around?

- Which groups encountered European explorers and conquistadors?

Types of Maps: Political, Physical, and Thematic

- What features/elements of a map are included on each?
- What purpose does each type of map serve?
- What information appears on certain types of maps but not others?

Functions of Government: Local, State, and Federal

- What are the major functions associated with each?
- What powers do certain levels have?
- What powers are denied at certain levels?

Relationship between North American countries: Canada, United States, and Mexico

- What common landforms do they have?
- Are their climates similar?
- How do these countries work together?

Types of Government: Republic, Monarchy, and Oligarchy

- How many people are in power in each type?
- What role do citizens play in each type of government?
- What is an example of a country with each type of government?

Qualities of Artistic Movements: Impressionism, Expressionism, and Surrealism

- What materials were used to create works of art in each movement?
- What general styles or techniques were used within each movement?
- Who are the famous artists affiliated with each movement?

Types of Tectonic Plates: Divergent, Convergent, and Transform

- What are examples of landforms caused by the various tectonic plate interactions?
- What natural disasters result from various tectonic plate interactions?
- How do humans adapt to deal with shifting of tectonic plates?

Role of Government in Economies: Communism, Socialism, and Market Capitalism

- Which allows for the most freedom of choice?
- Which has the most government involvement?
- Which is practiced in various countries?

Attributes of Founding Fathers: Washington, Jefferson, and Madison

- Where was each of them born?
- What role did each of them play in the American Revolution?
- What disagreements did they have?

Similarities and Differences of Colonial Conflict: Revolutionary War, French and Indian War, and War of 1812

- Who was involved in the conflict?
- Where did each conflict take place?
- What military technology or strategies were used in each conflict?

Major Figures of the Civil Rights Movement: Martin Luther King Jr., Rosa Parks, and Malcolm X

- How did each of these figures contribute to the civil rights movement?
- How did their methods differ?
- What beliefs did each figure hold?

Early River Valley Civilizations: Egypt, India, and Mesopotamia

- What lifestyles did each of these civilizations utilize?
- Where were each of these river valley civilizations geographically located?
- How did rivers provide and sustain life for each of these civilizations?

American Indian Tribes: Iroquois, Cherokee, and Seminole

- Where were each of these tribes geographically located?
- What type of jobs, diets, and ways of life did each tribe enact?
- What belief systems did each tribe have?

Sections of the U.S. Constitution: Preamble, Articles, and Amendments

- What do each of the sections have in common?
- Which lays out rights and functions of government?
- Which lays out rights and functions of citizens?

The use of the Venn diagram and the Triple Venn diagram are valuable learning tools. They align with one of the *Nine Instructional Strategies for Effective Teaching and Learning* as defined by Researchers at Mid-continent Research for Education and Learning (McREL). Identifying similarities and differences, as their research indicates, is one of the "strategies that are most likely to improve student achievement across all content areas and across all grade levels" (Marzano, Pickering, and Pollock 2001). Figure 6.5 is a student example of the Triple Venn diagram comparing the three branches of government.

Figure 6.5 Sample Triple Venn Diagram

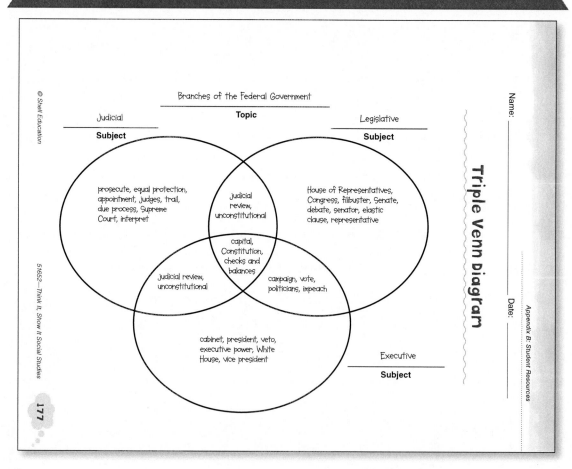

Compare-and-Contrast Sheets

The Triple Venn diagram shown in Figure 6.4 on page 109 allows for multiple comparisons and contrasts and is generally used with advanced students. With beginning students, have them first complete the *Compare-and-Contrast Text Plan* (Figure 6.6; reproducible on page 152). This sheet was introduced in Chapter 2. It can be used by both the teacher and students to prepare compare-and-contrast texts.

Figure 6.6 Compare-and-Contrast Text Plan (Beginning Students)

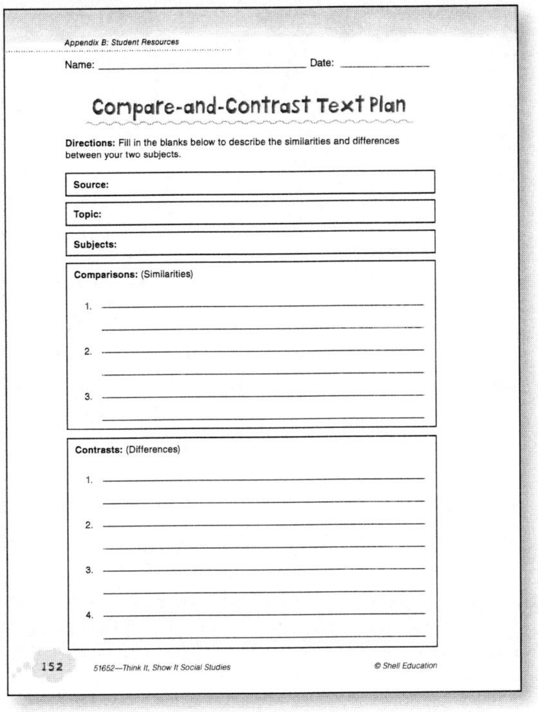
Appendix B: Student Resources

Name: ______________________ Date: __________

Compare-and-Contrast Text Plan

Directions: Fill in the blanks below to describe the similarities and differences between your two subjects.

Source:

Topic:

Subjects:

Comparisons: (Similarities)

1. ______________________
2. ______________________
3. ______________________

Contrasts: (Differences)

1. ______________________
2. ______________________
3. ______________________
4. ______________________

152 51652—Think It, Show It Social Studies © Shell Education

Two other sheets that may help students prepare to compare and contrast texts are shown in Figures 6.7 and 6.8 on page 116. Students can use the *Comparison Paragraph: How Subjects Are Alike* activity sheet (Figure 6.7; reproducible on page 178) to convert notes into paragraph format.

Figure 6.7 includes a student example based on Ann McGovern's picture book, *The Pilgrims' First Thanksgiving*. Students made comparisons between their own Thanksgiving celebrations and that of the Pilgrims. They then used this sheet to format their paragraphs.

Figure 6.7 Comparison Paragraph: How Subjects Are Alike

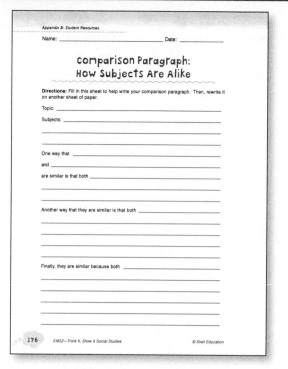

Blank Reproducible

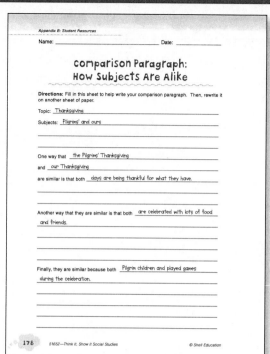

Student Example

Using the *Contrast Paragraph: How Subjects Are Not Alike* activity sheet (Figure 6.8; reproducible on page 179), students wre able to write second paragraphs.

Figure 6.8 Contrast Paragraph: How Subjects Are Not Alike

Blank Reproducible

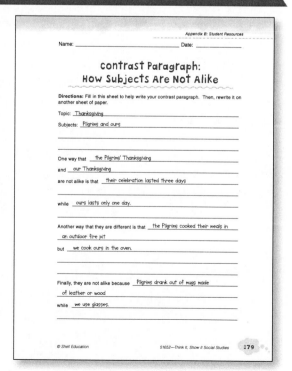

Student Example

Nouns, Verbs, and Adjectives

The *Nouns, Verbs, and Adjectives* activity sheet (Figure 2.7 on page 32; reproducible on page 180) can be used in a variety of ways. Its underlying objective is to collect and develop content- or domain-specific vocabulary while reinforcing grammatical parts of speech. There are three ways to have students use the sheet:

Three Ways to Use *Nouns, Verbs, and Adjectives*

1. While studying a topic, the class can generate an ongoing list of the nouns, verbs, and adjectives associated with the topic. These words can be posted on bulletin boards or copied by students in their Writer's Notebooks. Individual students or pairs of students can develop *Word Mastery* activity sheets (reproducible on page 182) or other vocabulary development strategies for learning critical words.

2. While individually researching topics, students can use the sheet to collect words in conjunction with their classroom or reading notes. They can refer to both when they begin writing their drafts.

3. Taking articles or selections of readings, students can be placed into groups of three. Then, students are each assigned a part of speech: nouns, verbs, or adjectives. First, students read the article or selection independently, looking for and identifying the three parts of speech. Emphasize that students should not be looking for any and all nouns, verbs or adjectives, but instead should be looking for specific ones directly associated with the article's topic:

   - **Nouns**—specific people, places, and things associated with the topic

   - **Verbs**—words that show action connected to the topic

   - **Adjectives**—words that describe people, places, or things associated with the topic

Then, working together, students share and discuss their findings, and fill out their *Nouns, Verbs, and Adjectives* activity sheet. Teachers can copy or post the article or text they want students to examine onto this blank sheet.

Team Searches: Nouns, Verbs, and Adjectives

Each participant takes one part of speech: nouns, verbs, or adjectives. Then, each participant reads the article individually, searching for and identifying the part of speech. Team Members share and discuss their findings and together fill out the *Nouns, Verbs, and Adjectives* sheet. An alternate approach has students working independently with an article or text and "coding" it. This means students would draw boxes around the nouns, draw circles around the verbs, and underline the adjectives.

Annotated Nouns, Verbs, and Adjectives Mentor Text: Battle of the Alamo (reproducible on page 125) shows an example of this activity.

The *Nouns, Verbs, and Adjectives* activity sheet can also be used with nonlinguistic sources. Prints, drawings, photographs, paintings, and illustrations are excellent primary sources for students to examine and generate words associated with their topics of study. Very often this can be used alongside an article or reading.

Mentor Texts

Mentor texts are written examples of texts that explicitly demonstrate the features of a specific type of writing. In social studies classrooms, mentor texts are vital instructional tools that guide students in analyzing the elements of particular types of writing. Utilizing close readings of a mentor text, students not only attend to the comprehension of the text, but also become familiar with the unique features of that text. This may include:

- What vocabulary and language do writers use with comparisons? Descriptions? Narratives? Arguments?

- What models can be utilized when presenting the "cause and effect" of events?

- What structures are used to organize persuasive arguments?

- What elements make up an effective informational or explanatory text?

In addition, mentor texts are used to highlight the fundamentals of expository prose:

- topic sentences and concluding statements

- elaboration of ideas through the use of details, facts, and examples

- varying sentence lengths

- precise word choices

- transition words

Mentor texts support what all writers and teachers know: for students to be successful with a particular type of writing, they must have read and investigated good examples of that particular type of writing. These examples provide students with blueprints from which they can model their own endeavors.

Included in this chapter are unannotated and annotated versions of mentor texts for different types of writing. Annotated texts explicitly show students the features of a particular type of writing while unannotated texts allow students to look for and identify the features. Teachers decide which version best fits the direction of their instruction. Digital copies of the unannotated and annotated texts are available within the digital resources. (See pages 199–200 for more information.)

Unannotated Block comparison: Two Houses of congress

The Congress of the United States government is responsible for enacting*, or making, laws. It is comprised of* two houses: the Senate and the House of Representatives. The men and women who make up these houses meet in the U.S. Capitol building in Washington, D.C., where they discuss, debate, and vote on bills. There are, however, important differences between the two houses.

The Senate is a body of 100 members, two from each state. Each member is elected for a six-year term. The vice president of the United States is the head of the Senate. He votes in the Senate in the case of a tie.

Like the Senate, the House of Representatives has a leader. He or she is called the speaker of the house and is elected by members of the House. The House of Representatives has 435 members, in contrast to the Senate's 100. In addition, instead of two senators from each state, the number of representatives from each state is determined by the population of the state. The larger the population of a state, the more representatives from that state. Also unlike senators, who are elected to serve for six years, representatives serve for only two years.

Through the design of the Constitution, senators and representatives are to represent the wishes of their constituents—those people who elected them—and are responsible for sending bills to the president. Before a bill can be signed by the president it must be approved by a majority of members in both houses of Congress.

*Working with new and more precise vocabulary: "enacting" & "is comprised of" (See *Word Mastery* sheet.)

Mentor Text: Block comparison

After the introduction of the subjects, the first half of the essay examines one of its subjects. The latter half is a comparison of the similarities and differences between the two subjects. A concluding paragraph is often used to complete the essay.

This mentor text demonstrates *topic* of the comparison essay, *subjects, words to compare*, and *words to contrast*.

Annotated Block Comparison: Two Houses of Congress

The Congress of the United States government is responsible for enacting*, or making, laws. It is comprised of* two houses: the Senate **[1st subject]** and the House of Representatives **[2nd subject]**. The men and women who make up these houses meet in the U.S. Capitol building in Washington, D.C., where they discuss, debate, and vote on bills. There are, however, important differences between the two houses **[topic sentence]**.

The Senate is a body of 100 members, two from each state. Each member is elected for a six-year term. The vice president of the United States is the head of the Senate. He votes in the Senate in the case of a tie.

Like **[words to compare]** the Senate, the House of Representatives has a leader **[similiarities between subjects]**. He or she is called the speaker of the house and is elected by members of the House **[difference between subjects]**. The House of Representatives has 435 members, in contrast **[words to contrast]** to the Senate's 100 **[difference between subjects]**. In addition, instead of two senators from each state **[difference between subjects]**, the number of representatives from each state is determined by the population of the state. The larger the population of a state, the more representatives from that state. Also unlike **[words to contrast]** senators, who are elected to serve for six years, representatives serve for only two years **[difference between subjects]**.

Through the design of the Constitution, senators and representatives are to represent the wishes of their constituents—those people who elected them—and are responsible for sending bills to the president. Before a bill can be signed by the president it must be approved by a majority of members in both houses of Congress.

*Working with new and more precise vocabulary: *"enacting"* & *"is comprised of"*
(See *Word Mastery* sheet.)

Mentor Text: Block Comparison

After the introduction of the subjects, the first half of the essay examines one of its subjects. The latter half is a comparison of the similarities and differences between the two subjects. A concluding paragraph is often used to complete the essay.

This mentor text demonstrates *topic* of the comparison essay, *subjects*, *words to compare*, and *words to contrast*.

Unannotated Point-By-Point Comparison: Two Houses of congress

The Congress of the United States government is responsible for enacting*, or making, laws. It is comprised of* two houses: the Senate and the House of Representatives. The men and women who make up these houses meet in the U.S. Capitol building in Washington, D.C., where they discuss, debate, and vote on bills. There are, however, important differences between the two houses.

The Senate is a body of 100 members, two from each state, as opposed to the number of House of Representatives members, which is determined by the populations of the states. The larger the population of a state, the more representatives from that state. Both houses have their leaders. The vice president of the United States is the head of the Senate. He votes in the Senate in the case of a tie. In contrast, the head of the House of Representatives is called the speaker of the house and is elected by members of the House. Although both senators and representatives are elected in their states for one or more terms, the lengths of the terms are different. A senator is elected for a six-year term, unlike representatives who serve for only two years.

Through the design of the Constitution, senators and representatives are to represent the wishes of their constituents—those people who elected them—and are responsible for sending bills to the president. Before a bill can be signed by the president it must be approved by a majority of members in both houses of Congress.

*Working with new and more precise vocabulary: *"enacting"* & *"is comprised of"* (See *Word Mastery* sheet.)

Mentor Text: Point-by-Point comparison

After the introduction of the subjects, individual comparisons between the subjects are presented as matched pairs throughout the body of the essay. A concluding paragraph is often used to complete the piece.

This mentor text demonstrates topic of the comparison essay, subjects, words to compare, and words to contrast.

Annotated Point-by-Point comparison: Two Houses of congress

The Congress of the United States government is responsible for enacting*, or making, laws. It is comprised of* two houses: the Senate **[1st subject]** and the House of Representatives **[2nd subject]**. The men and women who make up these houses meet in the U.S. Capitol building in Washington, D.C., where they discuss, debate, and vote on bills. There are, however, important differences between the two houses **[topic sentence]**.

The Senate is a body of 100 members, two from each state, as opposed to **[words to contrast]** the number of House of Representatives members, which is determined by the populations of the states. The larger the population of a state, the more representatives from that state **[difference between subjects]**. Both houses have their leaders. The vice president of the United States is the head of the Senate. He votes in the Senate in the case of a tie. In contrast **[words to contrast]**, the head of the House of Representatives is called the speaker of the house and is elected by members of the House **[difference between subjects]**. Although **[words to compare]** both senators and representatives are elected in their states for one or more terms, the lengths of the terms are different. A senator is elected for a six-year term, unlike **[words to contrast]** representatives, who serve for only two years.

Through the design of the Constitution, senators and representatives are to represent the wishes of their constituents—those people who elected them—and are responsible for sending bills to the president. Before a bill can be signed by the president, it must be approved by a majority of members in both houses of Congress.

*Working with new and more precise vocabulary: "*enacting*" & "*is comprised of*" (See *Word Mastery* sheet.)

Mentor Text: Point-by-Point comparison

After the introduction of the subjects, individual comparisons between the subjects are presented as matched pairs throughout the body of the essay. A concluding paragraph is often used to complete the piece.

This mentor text demonstrates topic of the comparison essay, subjects, words to compare, and words to contrast.

Unannotated Nouns, Verbs, and Adjectives: Battle of the Alamo

On February 23, 1836, the arrival of General Antonio Lopez de Santa Anna's army outside of San Antonio nearly caught the Texans and Tejanos by surprise. However, undaunted, they prepared to defend the Alamo and held out for 13 days against Santa Anna's vast army.

Williams B. Travis, the commander of the Alamo, sent forth couriers with pleas for help from communities in Texas. On the eighth day of the siege, a band of 32 volunteers from Gonzales arrived, bringing the number of defenders to nearly 200. Legend has it that Colonel Travis drew a line in the dirt and asked any man willing to stay and fight to step over it. It is believed that all did except one.

The Alamo was the key to the defense of Texas by attempting not to surrender its position to General Santa Anna. Among its garrison were the famed knife fighter, Jim Bowie, and frontiersman and former congressman from Tennessee, Davy Crockett.

The final assault came with columns of Mexican soldiers before daybreak on the morning of March 6. Cannons and rifles from inside the Alamo held off several attacks, but eventually the Mexican soldiers scaled the walls and rushed into the compound. They turned a captured cannon and blasted open the barricaded doors. The desperate struggle continued until the defenders were overwhelmed. By sunrise, the battle had ended, and Santa Anna entered the Alamo.

Through this valiant, but losing, effort, the Alamo has come to symbolize a heroic struggle against impossible odds. It represents a place where men made the ultimate sacrifice for freedom. The Alamo remains to this day hallowed ground and a shrine for Texas Liberty.

Mentor Text: Nouns, Verbs, and Adjectives

Read the article above. Code your paper as follows:

- Box nouns: specific people, places, and things associated with the topic

- Circle verbs: show action connected to the topic

- Underline adjectives: describe people, places, and things associated with the topic.

Repeated words need only to be marked once.

Annotated Nouns, Verbs, and Adjectives: Battle of the Alamo

On February 23, 1836, the arrival of General Antonio Lopez de Santa Anna's army outside of San Antonio nearly caught the Texans and Tejanos by surprise. However, undaunted, they prepared to defend the Alamo and held out for 13 days against Santa Anna's vast army.

Williams B. Travis, the commander of the Alamo, sent forth couriers with pleas for help from communities in Texas. On the eighth day of the siege, a band of 32 volunteers from Gonzales arrived, bringing the number of defenders to nearly 200. Legend has it that Colonel Travis drew a line in the dirt and asked any man willing to stay and fight to step over it. It is believed that all did except one.

The Alamo was the key to the defense of Texas by attempting not to surrender its position to General Santa Anna. Among its garrison were the famed knife fighter, Jim Bowie, and frontiersman and former congressman from Tennessee, Davy Crockett.

The final assault came with columns of Mexican soldiers before daybreak on the morning of March 6. Cannons and rifles from inside the Alamo held off several attacks, but eventually the Mexican soldiers scaled the walls and rushed into the compound. They turned a captured cannon and blasted open the barricaded doors. The desperate struggle continued until the defenders were overwhelmed. By sunrise, the battle had ended, and Santa Anna entered the Alamo.

Through this valiant, but losing, effort, the Alamo has come to symbolize a heroic struggle against impossible odds. It represents a place where men made the ultimate sacrifice for freedom. The Alamo remains to this day hallowed ground and a shrine for Texas Liberty.

Mentor Text: Nouns, Verbs, and Adjectives

Read the article above. Code your paper as follows:

- Box nouns: specific people, places, and things associated with the topic
- Circle verbs: show action connected to the topic
- Underline adjectives: describe people, places, and things associated with the topic.

Repeated words need only to be marked once.

Unannotated Persuasive Letter: House Rules

Dear Mom and Dad,

I have some questions. Are you concerned about the personal safety of your children? Do think that budgeting money is a good thing? Do you feel that our home needs to be a warm, inviting place? If you answered "yes" to any of these questions, read on.

I've been thinking about your long-standing policy of charging me a dollar for every light I might have innocently forgotten to turn off. Although I understand and appreciate your argument that monthly utility bills and light bulbs cost money, I believe the policy has some problems. First, consider that in the evenings I often need to go back and forth from my room to the family room and to the kitchen when I am doing my homework. If I turn off the lights each and every time, I run the risk of stumbling in the dark when I am trying to complete my homework. What if I injured myself? Consequently, there would be missed school and possibly doctor bills.

Consider my financial situation. With you charging me so much so often, my allowance is nearly gone on a weekly basis. How am I to learn to budget my money if I have none? I will need to ask you for loans rather than learning to budget on my own. In the big picture, is not the responsible use of money more important than punishing someone for forgetfulness?

Finally, there is my concern of the impression that a dark house gives to others. Let's say, for example, that I am in my room watching television and have faithfully turned off all other lights in the house. What if a neighbor wanted to pay a visit? Would they feel welcomed approaching such a dark and uninviting house? I think not.

So when you examine your "lights policy," I believe you will come to the conclusion that it is seriously flawed. When you consider, not only the dreary impression a dark house gives our neighbors and friends and the possible health issues, you will come to see that a better way of keeping utility bills down must be found.

Sincerely,
Your Loving Son

Mentor Text: Persuasive Letter

This mentor text demonstrates topic/issue, position, background information, reasons that support writer's position, persuasive words, presenting information words, and cause-and-effect words.

Annotated Persuasive Letter: House Rules

Dear Mom and Dad,

I have some questions. Are you concerned about the personal safety of your children? Do think that budgeting money is a good thing? Do you feel that our home needs to be a warm, inviting place? If you answered "yes" to any of these questions, read on.

I've been thinking about your long-standing policy of charging me a dollar for every light I might have innocently forgotten to turn off **[topic/issue]**. Although I understand and appreciate your argument that monthly utility bills and light bulbs cost money **[background information]**, I believe **[persuasive words]** the policy has some problems **[position]**. First **[presenting information word]**, consider in the evenings I often need to go back and forth from my room to the family room and to the kitchen when I am doing my homework. If I turn off the lights each and every time, I run the risk of stumbling in the dark when I am trying to complete my homework. What if I injured myself? Consequently, **[cause-and-effect word]** there would be missed school and possibly doctor bills **[reason that supports writer's position]**.

Consider my financial situation **[presenting information word]**. With you charging me so much so often, my allowance is nearly gone on a weekly basis. How am I to learn to budget my money if I have none? I will need to ask you for loans rather than learning to budget on my own **[reason that supports writer's position]**. In the big picture, is not the responsible use of money more important than punishing someone for forgetfulness?

Finally, there is my concern of the impression that a dark house gives to others. Let's say, for example, that I am in my room watching television and have faithfully turned off all other lights in the house. What if a neighbor wanted to pay a visit? Would they feel welcomed approaching such a dark and uninviting house? **[reason that supports writer's position]**. I think not. **[position]**.

So when you examine your "lights policy," I believe you will come to the conclusion that it is seriously flawed. When you consider, not only the dreary impression a dark house gives our neighbors and friends and the possible health issues, you will come to see that a better way of keeping utility bills down must be found.

Sincerely,
Your Loving Son

Mentor Text: Persuasive Letter

This mentor text demonstrates topic/issue, position, background information, reasons that support writer's position, persuasive words, presenting information words, and cause-and-effect words.

Unannotated Point-by-Point Argument: School Uniforms

By now it is well known that the School Board is considering that all students in the middle and high schools be required to wear school uniforms. The basis of the argument is that students often wear clothes that are inappropriate and do not represent our campuses well. Many students and parents, however, disagree with the idea and feel that there are other sides to the proposal that need to be considered.

Along with the inappropriateness, the Board argues that uniforms would assure decency in coed classrooms. Boys and girls do not need to be sitting next to provocatively dressed classmates. The question, however, is if not all students are dressing inappropriately, why should all students be required to wear uniforms. Wouldn't a school dress code enforced by the administration take care of the problem? It has also been suggested that school uniforms could help save families and students the cost of expensive brand name clothes. However, the dresses, slacks, shirts, and blazers of the uniforms are expensive, too. Furthermore, uniforms aren't going to stop students from wanting to wear the latest and most popular styles. Uniforms would only add additional clothing costs.

The Board has stated that school uniforms equalize students and lessen the problem of "cliques." Groups would not be formed according to those who can and cannot afford the expensive clothes. Cliques, however, are formed by much more than how students dress. Lifestyles, personalities, and common interests all influence how student groups are formed. Shouldn't the school work towards the acceptance of all students?

There is one last thing that needs to be considered in the discussion: Individuality. Uniforms would make all students look alike. Middle school students are at the stage where they are developing their unique personalities. If the Board is going to tell students how to dress, are they then going to tell students how to do their hair so everyone looks the same? While school uniforms are a suggested way to solve some problems, it is clear they may create even more problems.

Mentor Text: Point-by-Point Argument

After the introduction, all the opposing claims are explained and summarized before the writer presents his or her complete rebuttal. This mentor text demonstrates topic/issue, thesis statement, opposing claims, rebuttal statements, support statements.

Annotated Point-by-Point Argument: School Uniforms

By now it is well known that the School Board is considering that all students in the middle and high schools be required to wear school uniforms **[introduction of issue]**. The basis of their argument is that students often wear clothes that are inappropriate and do not represent our campuses well **[acknowledgement of opposing claims]**. Many students and parents, however, disagree with the idea and feel that there are other sides to the proposal that need to be considered **[thesis statement]**.

Along with the inappropriateness, the Board argues that uniforms would assure decency in coed classrooms **[1st opposing claim]**. Boys and girls do not need to be sitting next to provocatively dressed classmates. The question, however, is if not all students are dressing inappropriately, why should all students be required to wear uniforms **[rebuttal statement to 1st opposing claim]**. Wouldn't a school dress code enforced by the administration take care of the problem **[supporting statement]**? It has also been suggested that school uniforms could help save families and students the cost of expensive brand name clothes **[2nd opposing claim]**. However, the dresses, slacks, shirts, and blazers of the uniforms are expensive, too **[rebuttal statement to 2nd opposing claim]**. Furthermore, uniforms aren't going to stop students from wanting to wear the latest and most popular styles. Uniforms would only add additional clothing costs **[supporting statement]**.

The Board has stated that school uniforms equalize students and lessen the problem of "cliques." Groups would not be formed according to those who can and cannot afford the expensive clothes **[3rd opposing claim]**. Cliques, however, are formed by much more than how students dress. Lifestyles, personalities, and common interests all influence how student groups are formed **[rebuttal statement to 3rd opposing claim]**. Shouldn't the school work towards the acceptance of all students **[supporting statement]**?

There is one last thing that needs to be considered in the discussion: Individuality. Uniforms would make all students look alike. Middle school students are at the stage where they are developing their unique personalities. If the Board is going tell students how to dress are they then going to tell students how to do their hair so everyone looks the same? While school uniforms are a suggested way to solve some problems, it is clear they may create even more problems.

Mentor Text: Point-by-Point Argument

After the introduction, all the opposing claims are explained and summarized before the writer presents his or her complete rebuttal. This mentor text demonstrates topic/issue, thesis statement, opposing claims, rebuttal statements, support statements.

Unannotated Opposition/Rebuttal Argument: School Uniforms

By now it is well known that the School Board is considering that all students in the middle and high schools be required to wear school uniforms. The basis of their argument is that students often wear clothes that are inappropriate and do not represent our campuses well. Many students and parents, however, disagree with the idea and feel that there are other sides to the proposal that need to be considered.

Along with the inappropriateness, the Board argues that uniforms would assure decency in coed classrooms. Boys and girls do not need to be sitting next to provocatively dressed classmates. It has also been suggested that school uniforms could help save families the cost of expensive brand name clothes. Finally, the Board is making the case that school uniforms would equalize students and help lessen the problem of "cliques." Groups would not be formed according to those who can and cannot afford the expensive clothes.

While the concerns of the Board are reasonable, there are issues. First, it is clear that not all students dress inappropriately. Wouldn't a school dress code enforced by the administration take care of the problem? Saving money on the cost of clothes as suggested by the Board overlooks the fact that the dresses, slacks, shirts, and blazers of the uniforms are expensive too. Furthermore, uniforms aren't going to stop students from wanting to have the latest and most popular styles. Uniforms would only add additional clothing costs. Finally, cliques are formed by much more than how students dress. Lifestyles, personalities, and common interests all influence how student groups are formed. Shouldn't the school work towards the acceptance of all students?

There is one last thing that needs to be considered in the discussion: Individuality. Uniforms would make all students look alike. Middle school students are at the stage where they are developing their unique personalities. If the Board is going to tell students how to dress, are they then going to tell students how to do their hair so everyone looks the same? While school uniforms are a suggested way to solve some problems, it is clear they may create even more problems.

Mentor Text: Opposition/Rebuttal Argument

After the introduction, the opposing claims are explained and summarized before presenting a complete rebuttal. This mentor text demonstrates topic/issue, thesis statement, opposing claims, rebuttal statements, support statements.

Annotated Opposition/Rebuttal Argument: School Uniforms

By now it is well known that the School Board is considering that all students in the middle and high schools be required to wear school uniforms **[introduction of issue]**. The basis of their argument is that students often wear clothes that are inappropriate and do not represent our campuses well **[acknowledgment of opposing claims]**. Many students and parents, however, disagree with the idea and feel that there are other sides to the proposal that need to be considered **[thesis statement]**.

Along with the inappropriateness, the Board argues that uniforms would assure decency in coed classrooms **[opposing claim]**. Boys and girls do not need to be sitting next to provocatively dressed classmates. It has also been suggested that school uniforms could help save families the cost of expensive brand name clothes **[opposing claim]**. Finally, the Board is making the case that school uniforms would equalize students and help lessen the problem of "cliques" **[opposing claim]**. Groups would not be formed according to those who can and cannot afford the expensive clothes.

While the concerns of the Board are reasonable, there are issues. First, it is clear that not all students dress inappropriately **[opposing claim]**. Wouldn't a school dress code enforced by the administration take care of the problem **[supporting statement]**? Saving money on the cost of clothes as suggested by the Board **[opposing claim]** overlooks the fact that the dresses, slacks, shirts, and blazers of the uniforms are expensive, too **[rebuttal statement]**. Furthermore, uniforms aren't going to stop students from wanting to have the latest and most popular styles. Uniforms would only add additional clothing costs **[supporting statement]**. Finally, cliques are formed by much more than how students dress. Lifestyles, personalities, and common interests all influence how student groups are formed. Shouldn't the school work towards the acceptance of all students?

There is one last thing that needs to be considered in the discussion: Individuality. Uniforms would make all students look alike. Middle school students are at the stage where they are developing their unique personalities. If the Board is going tell students how to dress, are they then going to tell students how to do their hair so everyone looks the same? While school uniforms are a suggested way to solve some problems, it is clear they may create even more problems.

Mentor Text: Opposition/Rebuttal Argument

After the introduction, the opposing claims are explained and summarized before presenting a complete rebuttal. This mentor text demonstrates topic/issue, thesis statement, opposing claims, rebuttal statements, support statements.

Research Report: New Deal

Introduction

Gives the topic and its historical context. Includes a thesis statement or main idea of the paper.

The New Deal was the federal government's response to the Great Depression. On October 29, 1929, "Black Tuesday," the stock market crashed. People lost their investments and jobs, banks failed, and companies went bankrupt. When President Franklin Roosevelt took office in 1933, he instituted a series of acts and programs aimed at restoring the economy. These became known as the "New Deal." Each program had its own goals.

To begin with, to prevent people from continuing to withdraw money from the banks, President Roosevelt declared that banks would be closed for four days. Congress then passed the Emergency Banking Act which reorganized the banks and closed some of them. Banks were going to be secured by the federal government. This was an effort to create a level of confidence in people with the banking institutions.

Body

Thesis is explained and information and facts from writer's research is presented. Smooth progression and transition between the ideas of the paper.

His next move was to sign into law the Tennessee Valley Authority Act. This allowed the government to build dams on the Tennessee River. The dams were built to control flooding and generate hydroelectric power. Hydroelectric power provided inexpensive electricity for thousands of people.

In 1935 FDR began another project. He created the Works Progress Administration to give jobs to people. The program built post offices, bridges, schools, highways, and parks. In addition, it gave work to artists, writers, and musicians. The Civilian Conservation Corps Act gave jobs to three million young men building roads, planting trees, and putting fish into streams.

Equally important as a part of the New Deal was the Social Security Act of 1935. The aim was to lessen the risks of old age, poverty, unemployment, and the problems of widows and fatherless children.

Conclusion

Reiterates the thesis and gives the outcome of the historical context of the topic.

Eventually, as a result of the programs of the New Deal, the Great Depression was lessened. The economy recovered and people went back to work. The New Deal greatly improved the lives of many Americans.

Creative Excursions: Poetry

Creative excursions are learning opportunities that allow students to engage with social studies topics in unconventional forms. Ideas can be presented metaphorically. One example of a creative excursion is poetry. Writing poems enhances students' understanding of social studies by allowing them to explore the topic through poetic language and form. By writing poems, students can capture the essence of an idea. Poems can also open the door for non-language experiences. They can be illustrated, put to music, recorded, performed or dramatized, and presented in digital projects.

Two-Voice Poems

Two-voice poems are poems to be read by two voices. (See page 184 for an example.) They allow students to explore two different views, perspectives, and contributions of historical figures or populations of people. However, they work equally well with different but related concepts or topics in social studies. For instance, they can be written comparing and contrasting geographical regions, periods of history, movements, or concepts, such as supply and demand. Students can creatively personify non-human topics by giving them voices.

I am a prairie.

                                            I am a rainforest.

I have dense grasses and clusters of trees.

                                            I have tall, old growth trees.

We add to the beauty and variety of Earth.

Students assemble the content for their poems using a prewriting strategy, such as a Venn diagram (reproducible on page 176) or the *Compare-and-Contrast Text Plan* (reproducible on page 152). A reading of their final pieces can be performed in front of the class or can be a pre-recorded audio or video file. With this in mind, encourage students to write poems creatively with conversational, back and forth flavor. Page 134 includes another social studies example.

I am an earthquake.

Well, I'm called a tsunami.

We are both natural disasters.

I cause havoc under the earth's surface.
Shaking and swaying is my calling card.
I sometimes give little quivers now and then
to let people know that I'm always around.

My disturbance is under water. I'm recognized by
huge ocean or sea waves. I let the folks know I'm
coming by pulling back water from the shores.

But we are always unpredictable!

I get to cause buildings to collapse. Do you?

No, but I get to cause massive flooding.

Either way there is little time for people to escape.

When I come, people stay under
furniture such as a large table.

Heading for high ground is what I make the folks do.

**Together we make people think about what to do for safety.
For We Are Natural Disasters!**

Lunes

Poet Robert Kelly created the poetic form known as the "lune" as an alternative to the haiku. The Japanese pattern of the haiku counts syllables in each of its three lines. The lune counts words for its three lines:

Three words
Five words
Three words

In your classroom, put words from different units on small strips of paper or printed as a list on sheets. Students rearrange the word-strips around on their desks (or roam through the list on the sheet) until they find three words to start their poems. Then, they repeat the process but this time for five words, and repeat once more with three words. In the poem, they can use articles (an, and, and/or the), and prepositions (of, at, by, on, and/or to); however, other than any of the small words, they cannot repeat any word from the first line in the second line, nor can they repeat any word from the second line in the third line. Below is an example of a lune, written as part of a study of the Civil War.

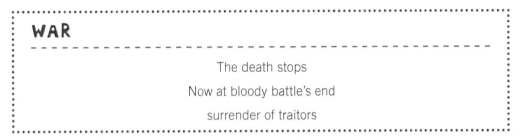

WAR

The death stops

Now at bloody battle's end

surrender of traitors

The *Lunes* sheet (Figure 8.1; reproducible on page 185) has the lune guidelines for students to work on and write their own lunes.

Figure 8.1 Lunes

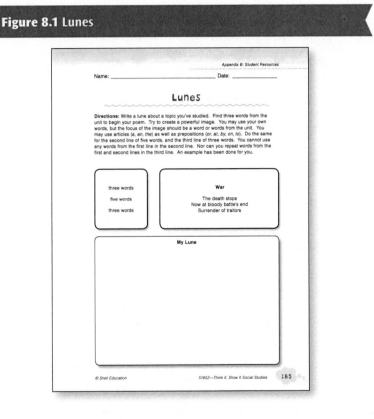

Cinquains

The cinquain can also be created with words from unit lists. With a cinquain, however, students are free to use any words. There are two basic patterns for cinquains:

Word-Count Cinquains

These cinquains increase in word count per line and end with a single word.

Title
One word
Two words
Three words
Four words
One word

Here is an example of a word-count cinquain.

> ## Desertification
>
> Desert
> Spread of
> By animal overgrazing
> Destroying vegetation and farming
> Erosion

Parts of Speech Cinquains

These cinquains use various parts of speech along with specified numbers of words per line to create poems.

Title
Adjectives (two words)
Gerunds, –ing words (three words)
Phrase (four words)
Synonym of or word connecting to the title

Chapter 8

Here is an example of a parts of speech cinquain:

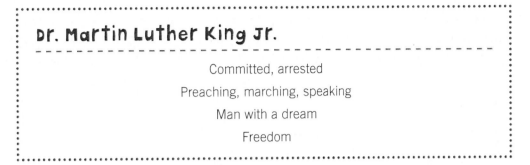

Dr. Martin Luther King Jr.

Committed, arrested

Preaching, marching, speaking

Man with a dream

Freedom

The *Cinquains* sheet (Figure 8.2; reproducible on page 186) has the cinquain guidelines for students to work on and write their own cinquains.

Figure 8.2 Cinquains

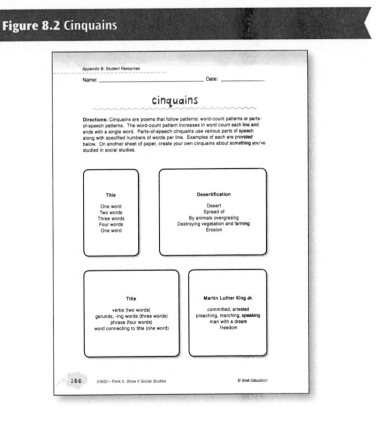

© Shell Education

51652—*Think It, Show It Social Studies*

137

Acrostics

An acrostic is a poetic form with a series of lines in which certain letters spell out a name, concept, or object. Usually, the letters are the first in each line, however, they do not have to be. The letters can be anywhere within the lines. Here are some examples:

Pearl Harbor

America was at **p**eace,

Attack was on D**e**cember 7, 1941,

It beg**a**n at 8:00,

Was ove**r** by 10:00,

At **l**east 2,400 Americans died.

Everything **h**ad changed,

18 **A**merican ships had sank or been damaged,

188 American ai**r**crafts had been destroyed,

But only 29 Japanese airplanes were lost,

It dem**o**lished The U.S. Navy,

President **R**oosevelt declared war on Japan.

The *Acrostics* sheet (Figure 8.3; reproducible on page 187) has the acrostics guidelines for students to work on and write their own acrostic poems.

Figure 8.3 Acrostics

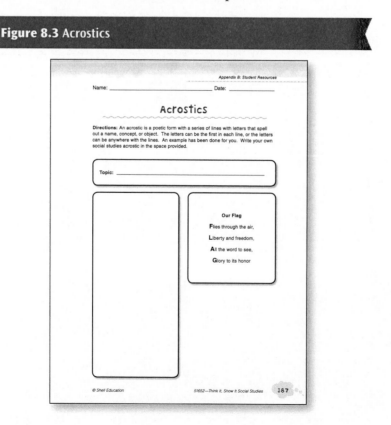

"I Believe" Poems

"I believe" poems are poems written as speeches where they express a historical or contemporary figure's beliefs. They are written in first person with each line beginning with "I believe." Here is an example using John Adams:

John Adams

I believe in America.
I believe that we should not be taxed without representation.
I believe in the Declaration of Independence, even if it means war.
I believe the purpose of government is the goal of the happiness of its citizens.
I believe in the self-government of the individual states.
I believe elections should be frequent for the rotation of those in office.
I believe public education should provide for the education of youth, especially of the lower class of people.
I believe military service builds the character of its citizens.
I believe in patriotism and freedom.
I believe in America.

The *"I Believe" Poems* sheet (Figure 8.4; reproducible on page 188) has the "I believe" poem guidelines for students to work on and write their own "I believe" poems.

Figure 8.4 "I Believe" Poems

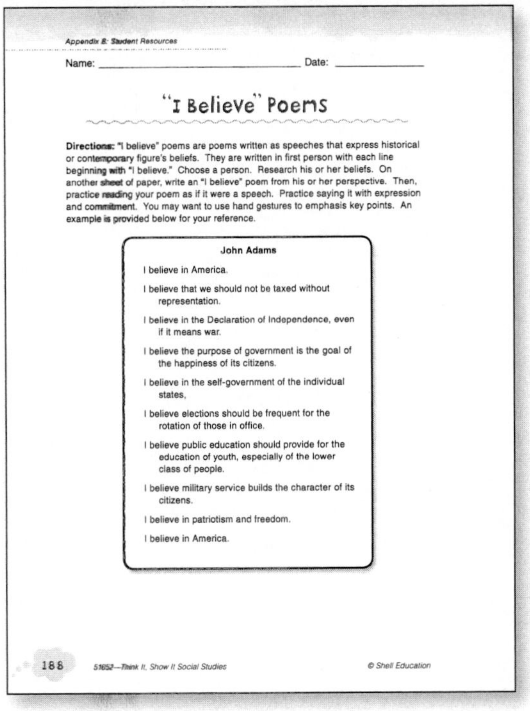

Appendix B: Student Resources

Name: ______________________ Date: __________

"I Believe" Poems

Directions: "I believe" poems are poems written as speeches that express historical or contemporary figure's beliefs. They are written in first person with each line beginning with "I believe." Choose a person. Research his or her beliefs. On another sheet of paper, write an "I believe" poem from his or her perspective. Then, practice reading your poem as if it were a speech. Practice saying it with expression and commitment. You may want to use hand gestures to emphasize key points. An example is provided below for your reference.

John Adams

I believe in America.
I believe that we should not be taxed without representation.
I believe in the Declaration of Independence, even if it means war.
I believe the purpose of government is the goal of the happiness of its citizens.
I believe in the self-government of the individual states.
I believe elections should be frequent for the rotation of those in office.
I believe public education should provide for the education of youth, especially of the lower class of people.
I believe military service builds the character of its citizens.
I believe in patriotism and freedom.
I believe in America.

188 51652—Think It, Show It Social Studies © Shell Education

"I Am from" Poems

"I am from" poems are poems written in first person where historical or contemporary figures discuss where they are from. Each line begins with "I am from." Here is an example using Abraham Lincoln:

Abraham Lincoln

I am from the woods of Kentucky.
I am from poor, rocky soil.
I am from one-room cabins.
I am from clothes made with the skins of animals.
I am from chores of chopping wood and collecting branches for fireplaces.
I am from bearskin bed covers.
I am from the hardships of farming families.

The *"I Am from" Poems* sheet (Figure 8.5; reproducible on page 189) has the "I am from" poem guidelines for students to work on and write their own "I am from" poems.

Figure 8.5 "I Am from" Poems

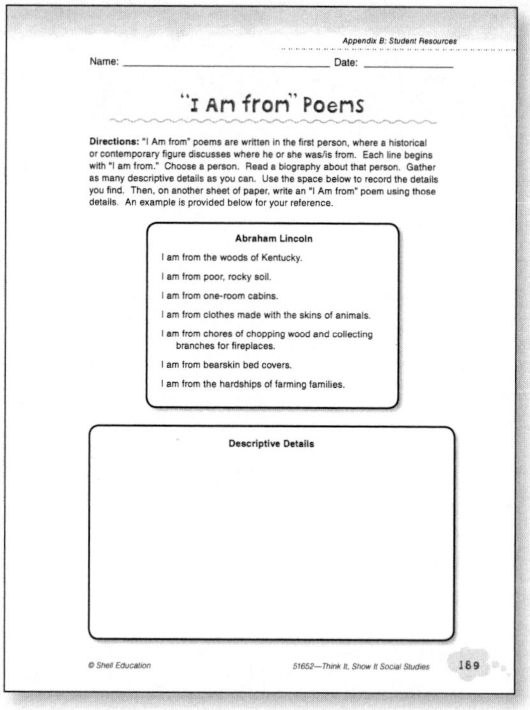

Appendix B: Student Resources

Name: ______________________ Date: __________

"I Am from" Poems

Directions: "I Am from" poems are written in the first person, where a historical or contemporary figure discusses where he or she was/is from. Each line begins with "I am from." Choose a person. Read a biography about that person. Gather as many descriptive details as you can. Use the space below to record the details you find. Then, on another sheet of paper, write an "I Am from" poem using those details. An example is provided below for your reference.

Abraham Lincoln

I am from the woods of Kentucky.
I am from poor, rocky soil.
I am from one-room cabins.
I am from clothes made with the skins of animals.
I am from chores of chopping wood and collecting branches for fireplaces.
I am from bearskin bed covers.
I am from the hardships of farming families.

Descriptive Details

© Shell Education 51652—Think It, Show It Social Studies 189

Personification Poems

Personification poems take inanimate objects and give them life-like or human qualities. Possible topics include:

- **Monuments:** The Statue of Liberty, Mount Rushmore, the Liberty Bell, and the Vietnam Memorial Wall

- **World Landmarks:** The Great Sphinx, the Roman Colosseum, the Great Wall of China, the Taj Mahal, and the Easter Island Statues

Students use what they have learned about the objects from their research as well as visuals, such as photographs or videos, to write their poems. Personification poems are always written in first person, and students should be encouraged to include pictures.

The Wall

Each day they come
    the young, the old
    many with tears in their eyes.

They come in wheelchairs
    or on crutches
    some in uniform.

Their faces read my many names
    until they stop
    pausing to look at one name.

Slowly, their hands reach up
    I can feel their fingers
    touch me.

Through the Wall we talk
    we say we miss each other
    we'll always remember each other.

Before they leave
    I tell them not to be sad
    I'll stand right here
    whenever they want to come back.

              by Greg Denman

The Vietnam Veterans Memorial, Washington, D.C.

References Cited

Anderson R. C., Freebody P. 1981. "Vocabulary knowledge." In *Comprehension and Teaching: Research Reviews*; edited by John T. Guthrie, 77–117, Newark, DE: International Reading Association.

Auman, Maureen. 1999. *Step Up to Writing: Basic, Practical, and Helpful Instruction for Writing Assignments, Assessments, and Everyday Writing Tasks.* Longmont: Sopris West.

Bogard, Jennifer M., and Maureen Creegan-Quinquis. 2013. *Strategies to Integrate the Arts in Social Studies.* Huntington Beach: Shell Education.

Bogard, Jennifer M., and Mary C. McMackin. 2015. *Writing Is Magic, Or Is It? Using Mentor Text to Develop the Writer's Craft.* Huntington Beach: Shell Education.

Burkhardt, Ross M. 2002. *Writing for Real: Strategies for Engaging Adolescent Writers.* Portland: Stenhouse Publishers.

Chapin, June R. 2012. *Elementary Social Studies: A Practical Guide.* Boston: Pearson Education.

Clark, Sarah Kartchner. 2007. *Writing Strategies for Social Studies.* Huntington Beach: Shell Education.

Conklin, Wendy. 2015. *Analyzing and Writing with Primary Sources.* Huntington Beach: Shell Education.

Dugan, Christine. 2010. *Strategies for Building Academic Vocabulary in Social Studies.* Huntington Beach: Shell Education.

Giese, Sarah D. 2006. *Hands-on History: Geography Activities.* Huntington Beach: Shell Education.

Hoyt, Jeff E., 1999. "Remedial Education and Student Attrition." *Community College Review* 27 (2): 51–72.

King, Stephen. *On Writing: A Memoir of the Craft.* New York: Simon & Schuster.

Marzano, Robert, Debra J. Pickering, and Jane E. Pollock. 2001. *Classroom Instruction that Works: Research-Based Strategies for Increasing Student Achievement.* Alexandria: Association for Supervision and Curriculum Development.

National Council for the Social Studies. 2013. *College, Career, and Civic Life (C3) Framework for Social Studies State Standards: Guidance for Enhancing the Rigor of K–12 Civics, Economics, Geography, and History.* Silver Spring, MD.

National Governors Association Center for Best Practices, Council of Chief State School Officers. 2010. *Common Core State Standards.* Washington, DC: National Governors Association for Best Practices, Council of Chief State School Officers. www.corestandards.org.

Shoob, Sara, and Cynthia Stout. 2008. *Teaching Social Studies Today.* Huntington Beach: Shell Education.

Name: _____ Date: _____

Thinking Through Your Writing

Directions: Use this to plan your writing.

Topic: _____

_____

_____

Purpose: _____

_____

_____

Questions My Writing Will Answer:

1. _____

_____

2. _____

_____

3. _____

_____

4. _____

_____

What Form Will My Writing Take?

_____

Name: _____ Date: _____

Add a Biographical Fact Planning Sheet

Directions: Choose a person. Write questions you want answered about him or her. Then, write the answers in the space provided.

> **My Person:**

> **Questions to Consider**

Name: _____ Date: _____

Adding Facts Planning Sheet

Directions: Choose a topic. Write questions you want answered about it. Then, write the answers in the space provided.

> **My Topic:**

> **Questions to Consider**

Name: _____ Date: _____

Revising My Writing

Directions: Write the purpose and topic of your paper. Answer the questions below to help evaluate your writing. Then, use your answers to revise your writing.

> **Write the purpose and topic of your paper.**
>
> _____
>
> _____
>
> _____

> **Think about these questions:**
>
> - Do I have a strong and clear opening/lead to my piece?
>
> - Have I stayed on topic? Is the main idea clear?
>
> - Is the information in my piece understandable with enough detail? Is it accurate? Do I need more?
>
> - Are there places where I need to give better, more thorough explanations?
>
> - Is there anything in the piece that doesn't talk about my topic and main idea? Do I need to take something out?
>
> - Do the different ideas follow a logical sequence in the presentation of the material? Do I need to move anything around? Are my transitions used effectively?

> **Continue by digging deeper with these questions:**
>
> - Have I used the key vocabulary of my topic correctly?
>
> - Have I used a variety of sentence structures: Some long; some short? Started in different ways?
>
> - Are my sentences smooth and easy to read aloud?
>
> - Have I chosen my words carefully? Are there better, more precise words I can use?
>
> - Are there words or phrases that are unnecessary and can be cut out?

100 Critical Spelling Words

again	although	answer	any	are
become	been	both	bought	catch
climbed	color	come	could	country
do	does	door	earth	edge
eight	enough	example	eyes	father
few	find	four	friend	from
give	great	group	have	heard
island	kind	knew	know	learn
listen	live	many	measure	most
mother	move	night	off	often
old	on	once	one	only
other	people	picture	piece	quickly
right	said	science	should	sign
snow	some	straight	stretch	sure
talk	their	there	they	though
thought	through	to	today	two
usually	walk	want	was	watch
water	were	what	where	who
women	word	work	world	would
write	wrote	you	young	your

Troublesome Homophones

allowed/aloud	ate/eight	aunt/ant
bizarre/bazaar	bolder/boulder	break/brake
cent/scent/sent	close/clothes	conch/conk
creek/creak	dear/deer	flew/flu/flue
foul/fowl	gait/gate	gene/jean
groan/grown	hair/hare	hole/whole
hour/our	lead/led	load/lode
main/mane	nose/knows	pear/pair
principal/principle	rap/wrap	right/write/rite
scene/seen	son/sun	straight/strait
tease/tees	tic/tick	vary/very
warn/worn	which/witch	would/wood

Name: _____ Date: _____

Partner Proofing

Directions: Pair up with another student. One of you assumes the role of "the reader." The other has the role of "the writer." The writer gives his/her paper to the reader and follows his/her responsibilities. The writer follows his/her responsibilities. Afterwards, change roles.

Reader's Responsibility

Reader: _____

While Reading

- notes words, sentences or ideas that give them—as readers—difficulty

- notes any problems with clarity—does it make sense?

- notes any mechanical errors or problems

- notes parts that are particularly well written

After Reading

- points out well-written sections

- explains and discusses any writing problems with the piece

- makes editing decisions with the writer

Writer's Responsibility

Writer: _____

After Reading

- listens to the reader's responses and concerns

- makes editing decisions with the reader

Name: _____ Date: _____

AGO Teaching Plan

Assignment

Topic _____

Purpose _____

_____

Format _____

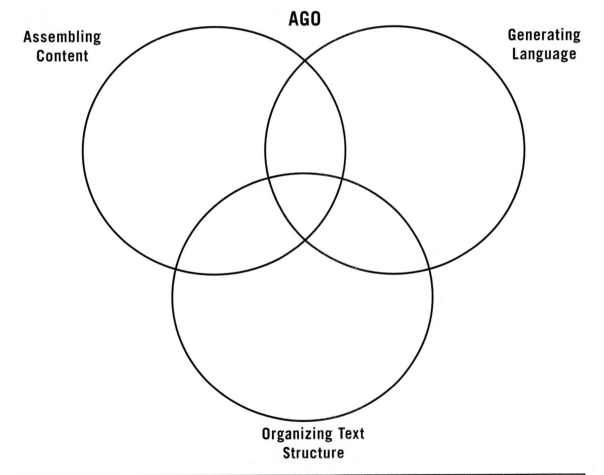

AGO

Assembling Content

Generating Language

Organizing Text Structure

Writing Process Elements

Creative Excursion

Name: _____ Date: _____

Compare-and-Contrast Text Plan

Directions: Fill in the blanks below to describe the similarities and differences between your two subjects.

Source:

Topic:

Subjects:

Comparisons: (Similarities)

1. _____
   _____

2. _____
   _____

3. _____
   _____

Contrasts: (Differences)

1. _____
   _____

2. _____
   _____

3. _____
   _____

4. _____
   _____

Name: _____ Date: _____

Sample compare-and-contrast Text

Two Houses of congress

The Congress of the United States government is responsible for enacting, or making, laws. It is comprised of two houses: the Senate and the House of Representatives. The men and women who make up these houses meet in the U.S. Capitol building in Washington, D.C., where they discuss, debate, and vote on bills. There are, however, important differences between the two houses.

The Senate is a body of 100 members, two from each state. Each member is elected for a six-year term. The vice president of the United States is the head of the Senate. He votes in the Senate in the case of a tie.

Like the Senate, the House of Representatives has a leader. He or she is called the speaker of the house and is elected by members of the house. The House of Representatives has 435 members in contrast to the Senate's 100. In addition, instead of two senators from each state, the number of representatives from each state is determined by the population of the state. The larger the population of a state, the more representatives from that state. Also, unlike senators who are elected to serve for six years, representatives serve for only two years.

Through the design of the Constitution, senators and representatives are to represent the wishes of their constituents—those people who elected them—and are responsible for sending bills to the president. Before a bill can be signed by the president it must be approved by a majority of members in both houses of Congress.

> **Directions:** Using a Venn diagram, fill in the similarities and differences between the subjects. Review the compare-and-contrast words below and underline those you find in the essay.

Words to Compare
- in the same way
- likewise, are alike
- similarly, are similar
- at the same time
- compared to
- both
- each of
- in common

Words to Contrast
- differences, difference between, differ
- opposite, as opposed to
- on the other hand
- in contrast
- instead of
- conversely
- while
- unlike

Name: _____ Date: _____

compare-and-contrast Sentences

Directions: Using what you learned from the unit, write compare-and-contrast sentences with words/phrases from the lists.

Words to Compare	Words to Contrast
• in the same way	• differences, difference between, differ
• likewise, as like	• opposite, as opposed to
• similarly	• on the other hand
• at the same time	• in contrast
• compared to	• instead of
• both	• conversely
• each of	• while
• in common	• unlike
• as well as	

1. _____

   _____

   _____

   _____

2. _____

   _____

   _____

   _____

3. _____

   _____

   _____

   _____

Name: _____ Date: _____

compare and contrast:
Search-and-Identify

Directions: Read the passage and follow the directions at the bottom of the sheet.

Directions

- Circle the topic of the essay.

- Underline its first subject with one line.

- Underline the second subject with two lines.

- Draw a box around each of the differences between the subjects.

- Place a check on words to contrast and words to compare.

Name: _____ Date: _____

Student Opinion Paper Guide

Directions: After reading the topic question, follow the directions at the bottom of the page to write your opinion paper.

Topic Question _____

_____

_____

_____

_____

_____

_____

_____

_____

_____

_____

_____

1. **Opinion Sentence:** Write an opening sentence clearly stating your opinion (what you think). Include key words from the Topic Question with your sentence. Use one of these sentence stems to start: *I think, I don't think, I believe, I don't believe,* or *In my opinion.*

2. **Reason/Evidence Sentences:** Continue by writing two or more sentences with reasons that support your opinion (why you think what you think). Use one of these transition (linking) words with each sentence: *first, second, also, next, finally,* or *in addition.*

3. **Summary Sentence:** Finish by writing a sentence where you summarize the reasons for your opinion.

Name: _____ Date: _____

Topic, Issue, and Position Statement Planning Grid

Directions: Complete this activity sheet to outline your opinion.

Topic: _____

_____

Issue: _____

_____

Position Statement: _____

_____

Background Information: _____

_____

_____

Reasons I Support My Position:

1. _____

_____

2. _____

_____

_____

3. _____

_____

How to Structure a Persuasive Essay

Begin (introduction):

- engaging topic sentence(s)
- explanation of the issue
- clearly stated writer's position on the issue

Helpful Words and Phrases

- in my opinion
- I believe
- it is my belief that
- from my point of view
- I question whether
- I (dis)agree
- I maintain that
- there is no doubt that

Continue (body of the essay):

- reasons to support writer's position
- examples, logic, and/ or evidence to support each point

Helpful Words and Phrases

- first
- to begin with
- next
- because
- since
- for example
- finally
- last
- consequently
- in addition
- according to
- I believe
- in my opinion
- in my experience
- although
- despite
- on the other hand
- still
- moreover
- besides
- similarly
- further
- for example
- in fact
- as evidence
- for instance
- in support of this
- I believe

Finish (conclusion):

- restatement of the issue and the writer's position (try not to use the exact wording you used in your Introduction)
- reiteration of key or most powerful points of writer's reasons and facts (again trying not to use the same wording used in the body of your essay)
- ending with a strong summarizing statement(s), possibly making a powerful personal or emotional appeal

Helpful Words and Phrases

- to sum up
- in short
- in brief
- as you can see
- as I have explained
- in summation
- in other words
- in conclusion
- in any event
- as I have noted
- obviously
- as you can see
- without a doubt

Name: _____ Date: _____

Opposing Reasons/Your Argument Planning Sheet

Directions: Complete the activity sheet to record opposing reasons and your argument against those reasons.

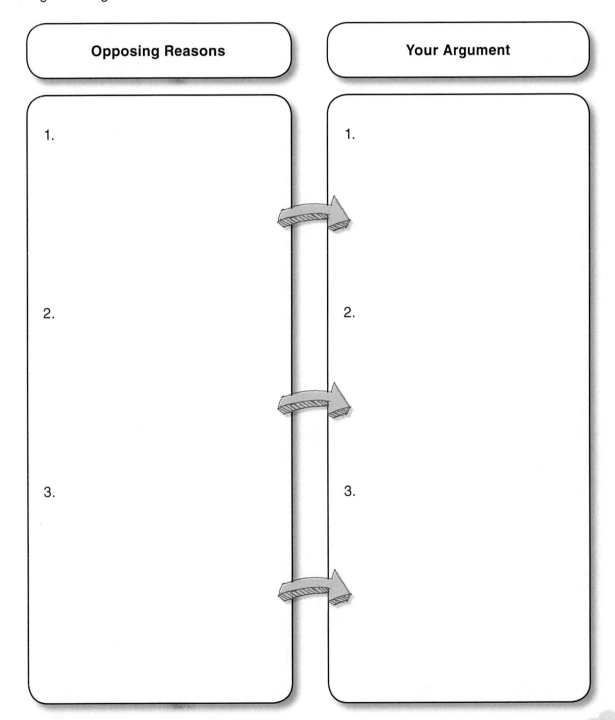

Opposing Reasons	Your Argument
1.	1.
2.	2.
3.	3.

Name: _____ Date: _____

Argument T-chart

Directions: After determining your topic issue and position, fill in the T-chart with your opposing claims and rebuttals.

Topic _____

Issue _____

Position _____

Opposing Claims	Rebuttal

Name: _____ Date: _____

Explanatory Text Planning Web

Directions: Write your topic in the center space. Add details and additional information in the appropriate spaces.

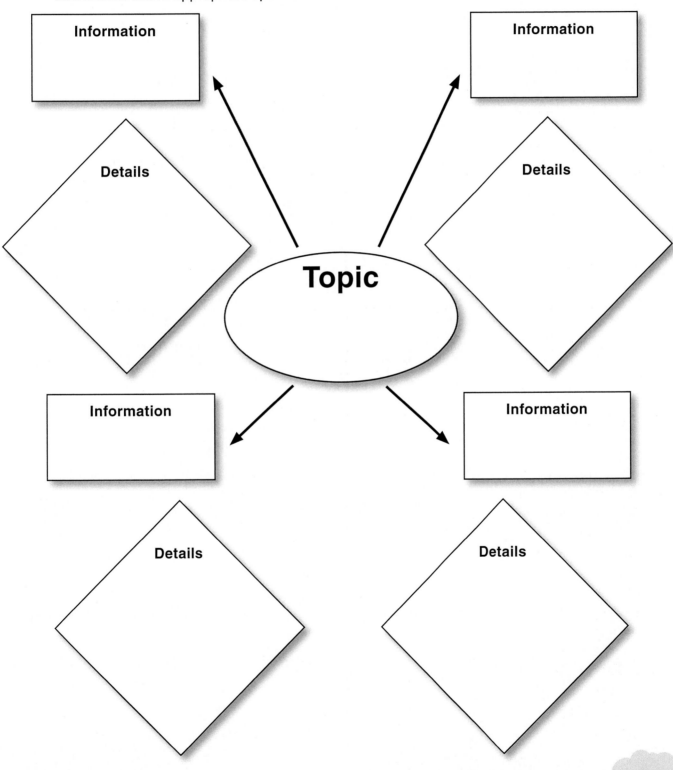

Name: _____ Date: _____

Explanatory Text Planning Chart

Directions: Write your topic at the top of the activity sheet. Add details and additional information in the appropriate spaces below.

Topic

Information

Information

Details

Details

Name: _____ Date: _____

Pick a Great Combination of Transition Words

Beginning	Middle	End
first	another way	third
one way	second	the best
one example	third	finally
first of all	next	last
a good	in addition	in conclusion
a poor	along with	the final
to begin with	then	equally as important
initially	a better	a final way
	also	
	a worse	
	besides	
	one other	

Remember

Use, vary, and bury your transition words.

Name: _____ Date: _____

Thesis Web

Directions: Use this sheet to develop your thesis. Additional circles can be added.

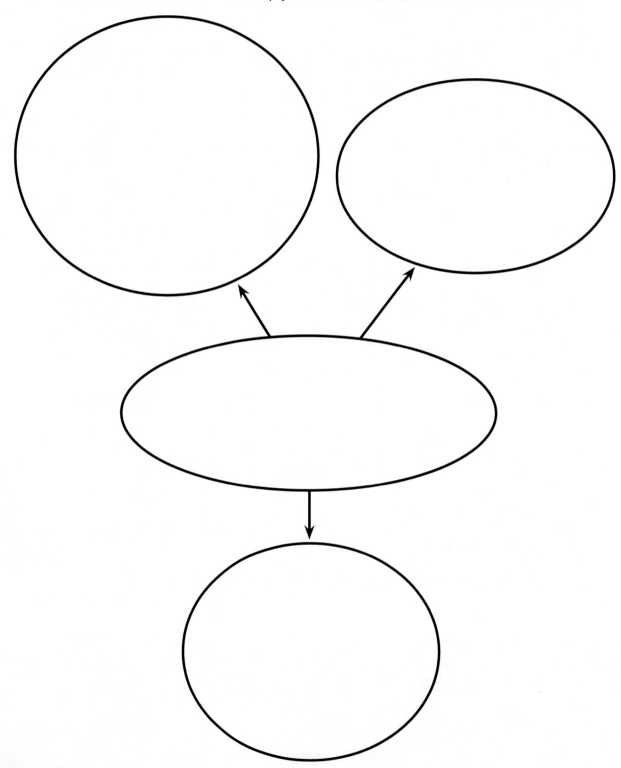

Name: _____ Date: _____

Descriptive Writing

Directions: Write your topic on the line below. Write details and images in the available space. Use as many senses as you can.

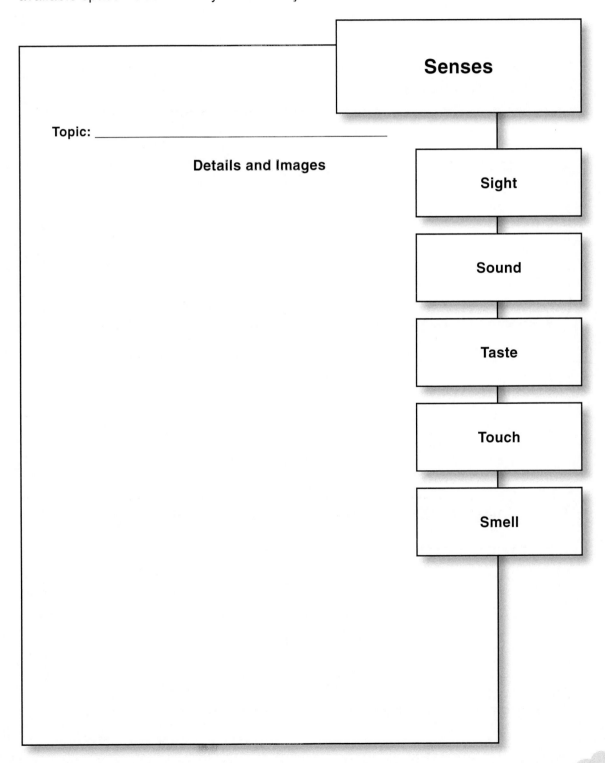

Topic: _____

Details and Images

Senses

Sight

Sound

Taste

Touch

Smell

Name: _____ Date: _____

Cause and Effect

Directions: Use this sheet to record the causes and effects found on your topic.

> To determine causes, ask: Why did this happen? or What are causes? or
> What are the factors that cause _____ ?
>
> To determine effects, ask: What happened because of this? or What is the effect
> or result? or What are the factors that resulted from this cause?

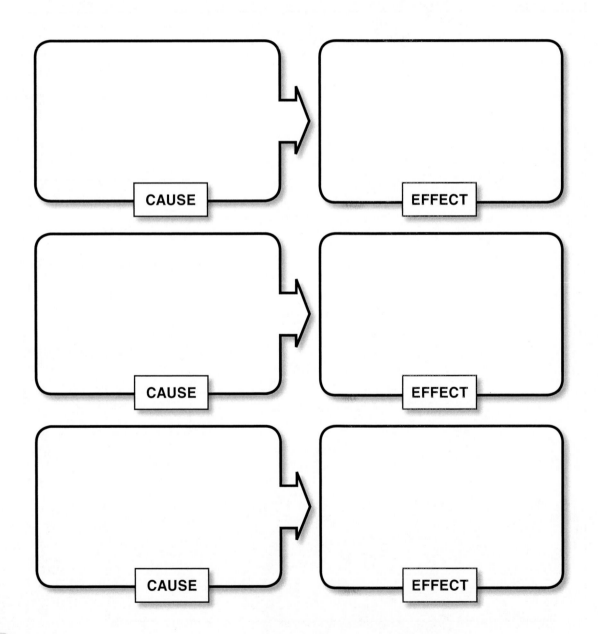

Name: _____ Date: _____

Cause-and-Effect Sentences

Directions: Use this sheet to write cause first and effect first sentences.

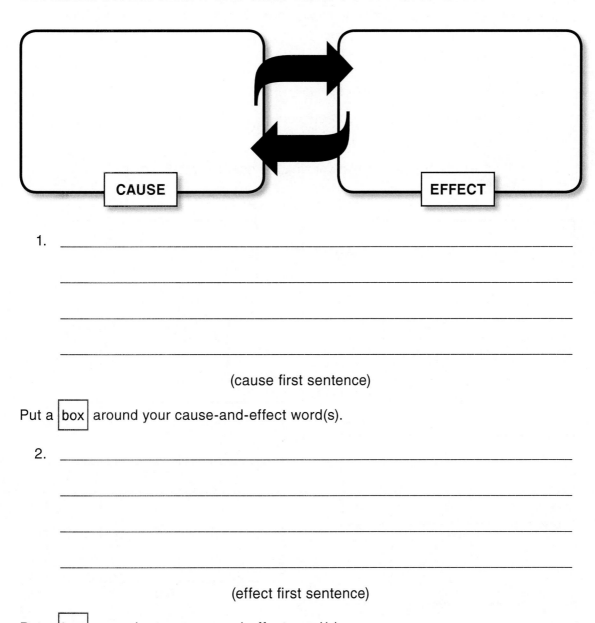

CAUSE

EFFECT

1. _____

_____

_____

_____

(cause first sentence)

Put a box around your cause-and-effect word(s).

2. _____

_____

_____

_____

(effect first sentence)

Put a box around your cause-and-effect word(s).

Cause-and-Effect Words
because, a reason for this, so, when, as a result, since, consequently, if, due to

Name: _____ Date: _____

Cause-and-Effect Mapping

Directions: Draw and fill in cause-and-effect boxes and arrows that map out the cause and effects and the subsequent events found in the article. Label each box either *cause* or *effect*.

Look for:

- single causes leading to a single effect/event
- single causes leading to multiple effect/events
- multiple causes leading to a single effect/event
- one event causing another effect/event which triggers another which causes another

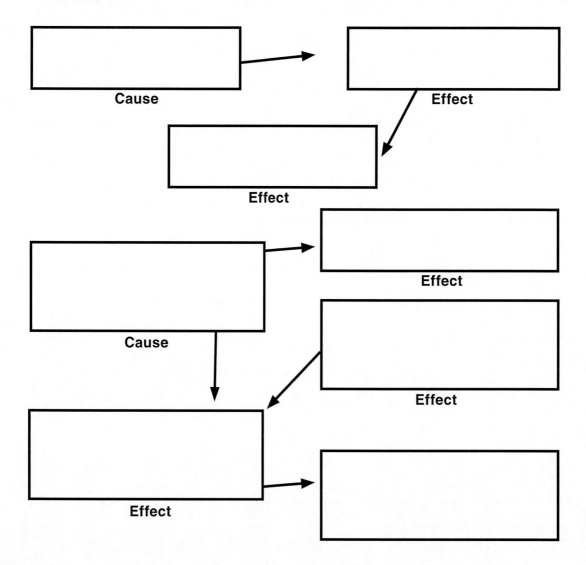

Name: _____ Date: _____

Summary/Information Web

Directions: Fill in the circles.

Summary

- What information is central to the overall meaning of the passage?

- What supporting details are necessary for understanding the information?

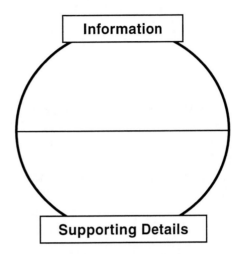

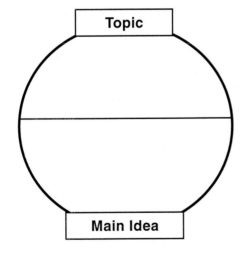

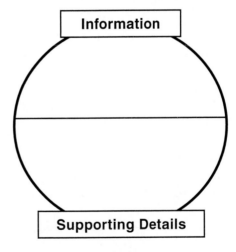

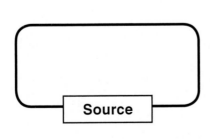

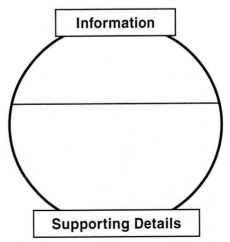

Name: _____ Date: _____

Writing Graph Summary Statements

Directions: Circle the words and fill in the blanks to complete this sheet using your graph for reference.

The   bar graph

         data table   shows

         line graph   tells me

         circle graph   demonstrates   that

_____

_____.

(Data Interpretation: What I know)

I know because _____

_____.

         But

         While

         Whereas

         In contrast to_____

_____.

(Evidence Statement: How I know it)

Additional evidence statements can begin with transition words, such as *also* or *another way*.

Name: _____ Date: _____

Graph Sentences

Directions: Circle the words and fill in the blanks to complete this sheet using your graph for reference.

As   indicated

       suggested

       shown

by the graph _____

                    (source)

_____

Positive	**Negative**	**No Difference**
is higher	is lower	is the same as
is the highest	is the lowest	showed no difference
climbed	fall	showed no increase or decrease
rose	declined	is similar to
increased	dipped	

than

from

compared to

_____

Name: _____ Date: _____

connection Sentences

Directions: Use the space below to brainstorm words or phrases that are significant to the topic or person you are studying. Then, fill in the blanks to create your connection sentences.

Topic: _____

_____ is connected to _____

because _____

_____

_____

Topic: _____

_____ is connected to _____

because _____

_____

_____

Name: _____ Date: _____

Vocabulary Pre-Test

1. **Directions:** Match the words to the definitions.

Words	Definitions

2. **Directions:** Find sentences in the book that explains or confirms that you had the correct matches.

_____

_____

_____

_____

_____

Name: _____ Date: _____

Pre-Reading Vocabulary Assessment sample

Directions: You will be reading an article: "Natural Disasters Information: Blizzard." Before reading the article, assess your knowledge of the words below.

1. Check box A if you have no knowledge of the word. In other words you haven't got a clue!

2. Check box B if you have seen or heard the word but can't define it yet.

3. Write out a "working" definition of what you believe the word to mean in box C.

	A	B	C
blizzard			wind, heavy snow storm
high pressure system		✓	
lake-effect snow	✓		
low-pressure system		✓	
drifts			blown deep snow

Name: _____ Date: _____

Pre-Reading Vocabulary Assessment

Directions: You will be reading an article: _____.
Before reading the article, assess your knowledge of the words below.

1. Check box A if you have no knowledge of the word. In other words you haven't got a clue!

2. Check box B if you have seen or heard the word, but can't define it yet.

3. Write out a "working" definition of what you believe the word to mean in box C.

	A	B	C

Name: _____ Date: _____

Venn Diagram

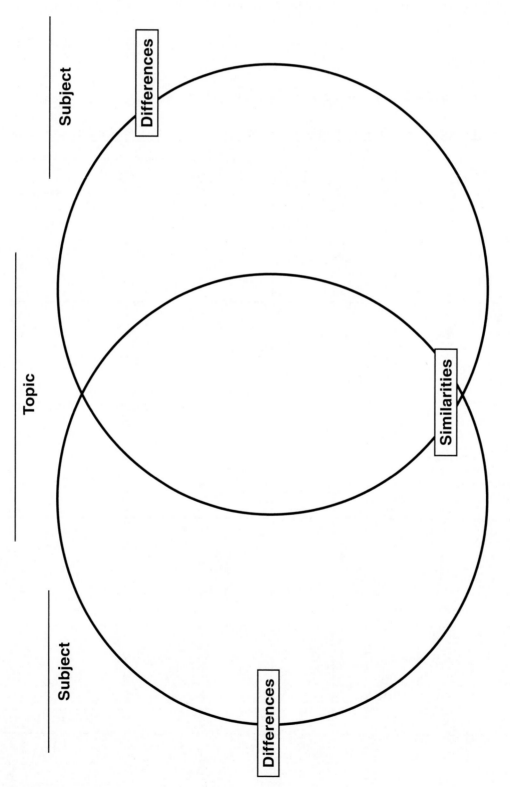

Subject

Differences

Topic

Similarities

Subject

Differences

Name: _____ Date: _____

Triple Venn Diagram

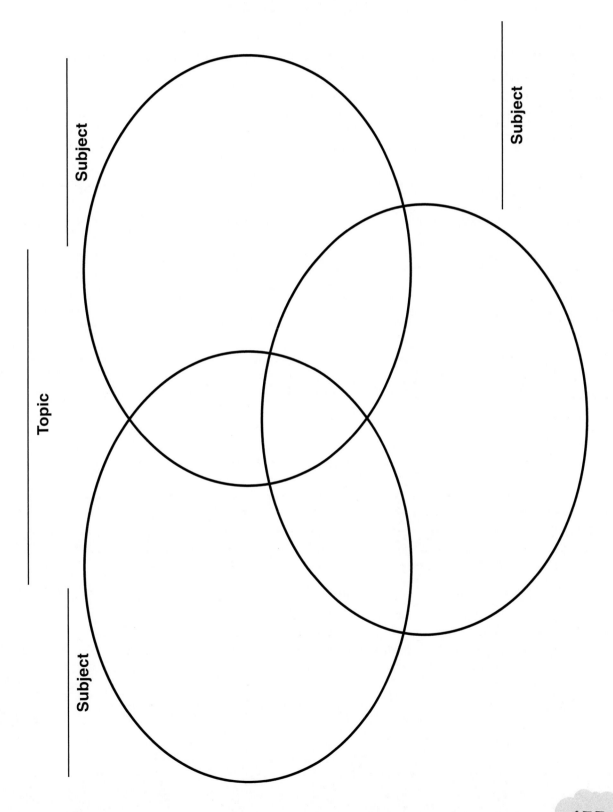

Name: _____ Date: _____

comparison Paragraph: How Subjects Are Alike

Directions: Fill in this sheet to help write your comparison paragraph. Then, rewrite it on another sheet of paper.

Topic: _____

Subjects: _____

_____

_____

One way that _____

and _____

are similar is that both _____

_____

_____

Another way that they are similar is that both _____

_____

_____

_____

_____

Finally, they are similar because both _____

_____

_____

_____

_____

_____

Name: _____ Date: _____

contrast Paragraph: How Subjects Are Not Alike

Directions: Fill in this sheet to help write your contrast paragraph. Then, rewrite it on another sheet of paper.

Topic: _____

Subjects: _____

_____

_____

One way that _____

and _____

are not alike is that _____

_____

while _____

_____

Another way that they are different is that _____

_____

but _____

_____

_____

Finally, they are not alike because _____

_____

while _____

_____

Name: _____ Date: _____

Nouns, Verbs, and Adjectives

Directions: Write your topic in the center space. Add details that match the description in each additional box.

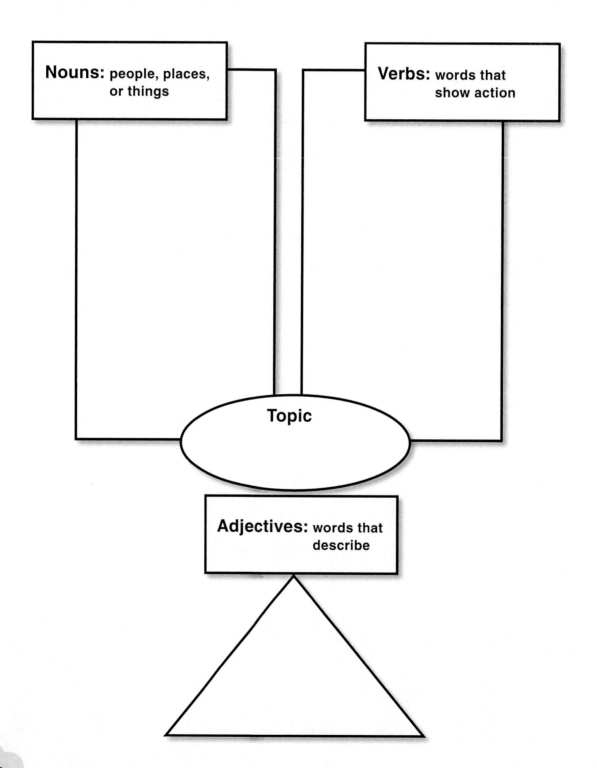

Name: _____ Date: _____

Nouns, Verbs, and Adjectives Text

Directions: Read the article above. Code your paper as follows:

- Box nouns: specific people, places, and things associated with the topic

- Circle verbs: show action connected to the topic

- Underline adjectives: describe people, places, and things associated with the topic.

Repeated words need only to be marked once.

Name: _____ Date: _____

Word Mastery

Directions: Fill in the missing information in each space below.

1. Word	2. Part of Speech

3. Dictionary Definition

4. Synonym	5. Antonym

6. Association

7. Different Context

Name: _____ Date: _____

Two-Voice Poems

Directions: Choose two points of view. Research what they have in common and how they differ. In the "First Voice" box, write what is unique to one of the points of view. Do the same in the "Second Voice" box. Write what the two views have in common in the "Both Voices" box. Then, on another sheet of paper, use the ideas in the boxes to compose your two-voice poem. Use the word "I" with the first and second voices and the word "we" when the voices talk together. Be creative, have fun, and make it sound as though the voices are talking back and forth to one another.

First Voice	**Second Voice**

Both Voices

Two-Voice Poems: Senate and House of Representatives

I am a senator. I work in the Senate.

> I am a representative. You'll find me in the House of Representatives.

**We are the legislative branch of the U.S. government.
We are responsible for making laws.**

There are 100 members in my house. We are fair. Two for every state.

> We have 435 members. The population of the state determines how many representatives each state gets. It works like this: The larger the population, the more representatives!

**All together, we form Congress and meet in the
Capitol building in Washington, D.C.**

I'm elected for a six-year term.

> Really? We are elected for only two years.

The vice president of the United States is our leader. He or she gets to vote if there is a tie in the Senate.

> We call the leader of our house the speaker of the house.

**Both of us have to discuss, debate, and vote on bills.
But bills have to be signed by the president before they become laws.**

Name: _____ Date: _____

Lunes

Directions: Write a lune about a topic you've studied. Find three words from the unit to begin your poem. Try to create a powerful image. You may use your own words, but the focus of the image should be a word or words from the unit. You may use articles (*a*, *an*, *the*) as well as prepositions (*or*, *at*, *by*, *on*, *to*). Do the same for the second line of five words, and the third line of three words. You cannot use any words from the first line in the second line. Nor can you repeat words from the first and second lines in the third line. An example has been done for you.

---

three words

five words

three words

War

The death stops
Now at bloody battle's end
Surrender of traitors

My Lune

Name: _____ Date: _____

cinquains

Directions: Cinquains are poems that follow patterns: word-count patterns or parts-of-speech patterns. The word-count pattern increases in word count each line and ends with a single word. Parts-of-speech cinquains use various parts of speech along with specified numbers of words per line. Examples of each are provided below. On another sheet of paper, create your own cinquains about something you've studied in social studies.

Title

One word
Two words
Three words
Four words
One word

Desertification

Desert
Spread of
By animals overgrazing
Destroying vegetation and farming
Erosion

Title

verbs (two words)
gerunds, -ing words (three words)
phrase (four words)
word connecting to title (one word)

Martin Luther King Jr.

committed, arrested
preaching, marching, speaking
man with a dream
freedom

Name: _____ Date: _____

Acrostics

Directions: An acrostic is a poetic form with a series of lines with letters that spell out a name, concept, or object. The letters can be the first in each line, or the letters can be anywhere with the lines. An example has been done for you. Write your own social studies acrostic in the space provided.

Topic: _____

Our Flag

Flies through the air,

Liberty and freedom,

All the word to see,

Glory to its honor

Name: _____ Date: _____

"I Believe" Poems

Directions: "I believe" poems are poems written as speeches that express historical or contemporary figure's beliefs. They are written in first person with each line beginning with "I believe." Choose a person. Research his or her beliefs. On another sheet of paper, write an "I believe" poem from his or her perspective. Then, practice reading your poem as if it were a speech. Practice saying it with expression and commitment. You may want to use hand gestures to emphasis key points. An example is provided below for your reference.

John Adams

I believe in America.

I believe that we should not be taxed without representation.

I believe in the Declaration of Independence, even if it means war.

I believe the purpose of government is the goal of the happiness of its citizens.

I believe in the self-government of the individual states,

I believe elections should be frequent for the rotation of those in office.

I believe public education should provide for the education of youth, especially of the lower class of people.

I believe military service builds the character of its citizens.

I believe in patriotism and freedom.

I believe in America.

Name: _____ Date: _____

"I Am from" Poems

Directions: "I Am from" poems are written in the first person, where a historical or contemporary figure discusses where he or she was/is from. Each line begins with "I am from." Choose a person. Read a biography about that person. Gather as many descriptive details as you can. Use the space below to record the details you find. Then, on another sheet of paper, write an "I Am from" poem using those details. An example is provided below for your reference.

Abraham Lincoln

I am from the woods of Kentucky.

I am from poor, rocky soil.

I am from one-room cabins.

I am from clothes made with the skins of animals.

I am from chores of chopping wood and collecting branches for fireplaces.

I am from bearskin bed covers.

I am from the hardships of farming families.

Descriptive Details

Name: _____ Date: _____

The Editing Process

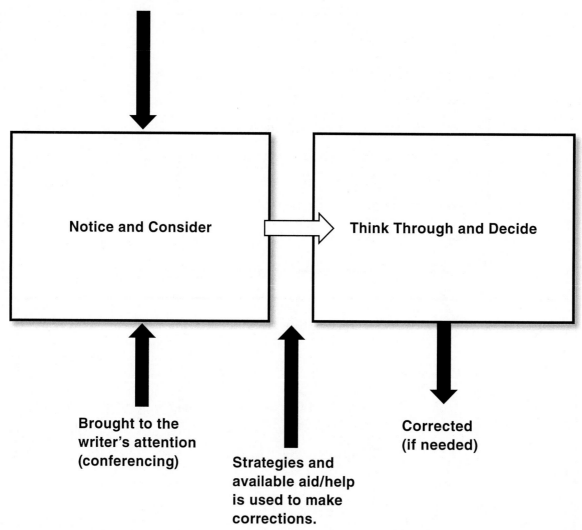

High-Glare Errors

- typical writers' problems
- personal error patterns

Notice and Consider

Think Through and Decide

Brought to the writer's attention (conferencing)

Strategies and available aid/help is used to make corrections.

Corrected (if needed)

Introduction, Body, Conclusion

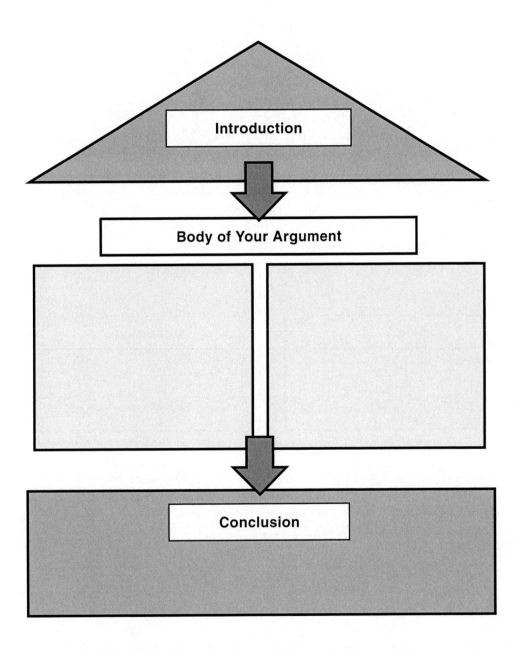

Paragraph Mobile

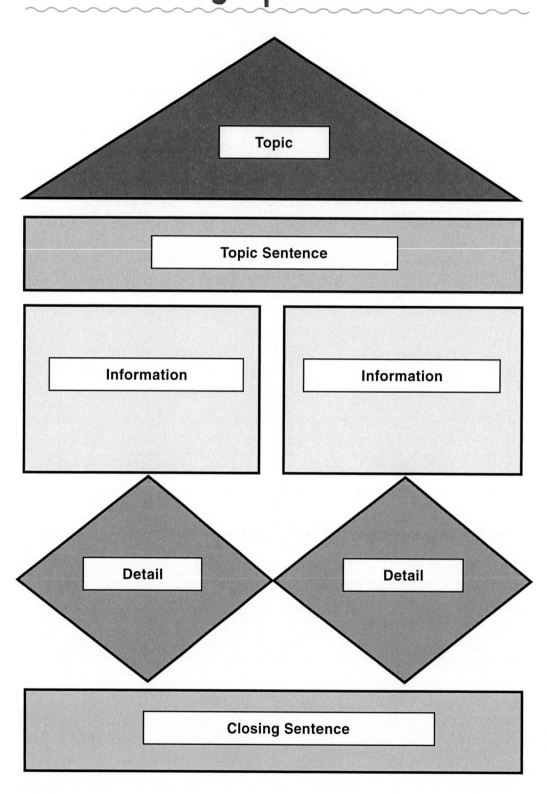

Five Paragraph Essay

Introduction

Uses essay question for main idea; gives historical context; presents thesis statement; and makes reference to topics of body paragraphs.

Body Paragraph #1

Begins with a topic sentence; presents and cites evidence from documents and social studies knowledge; and has smooth and effective transitions between ideas.

Body Paragraph #2

Begins with a topic sentence; presents and cites evidence from documents and social studies knowledge; and has smooth and effective transitions between ideas.

Body Paragraph #3

Begins with a topic sentence; presents and cites evidence from documents and social studies knowledge; and has smooth and effective transitions between ideas.

Conclusion

Briefly reiterates historical context and essay question; sums up main idea; restates thesis to conclude essay.

Compare-and-Contrast Rubric

	10	5	1
Content	Includes similarities and differences of subjects that are accurate and complete. Where appropriate, specific, supporting details and examples are given. Contains no irrelevant information.	Information is generally accurate. Many of the similarities and differences between the subjects are given but not with a complete discussion. Lacks sufficient elaboration.	Lacks accurate and complete information of the similarities and differences of subjects. Possibly irrelevant information is included.
Organization and Structure	Introduction and conclusion are well written and effective. Paper follows one of the comparison patterns. Body paragraphs include topic sentences and follow logical progression of ideas. Transition words provide smooth movement from one idea to the next.	Paper has introduction and conclusion, but the body isn't clearly organized with one of the comparison patterns. Body paragraphs lack definitive topic sentences. Some transitions work, but the connections between other ideas are unclear.	Lacks or has poorly written introduction and/or conclusion. Paper doesn't follow one of the comparison patterns. There is an Illogical presentation of ideas and/or weak transitions from one idea to the next.
Language	Correctly and accurately uses domain-specific and precise vocabulary. Includes compare-and-contrast sentences.	There is a limited use of domain-specific and precise vocabulary and compare-and-contrast sentences.	There is no use or inaccurate use of domain-specific vocabulary and compare-and-contrast sentences.
Grammar, Usage, Mechanics, and Spelling	Paper has only a few errors that do not distract or impede meaning.	There are several errors that potentially distract from the reading of the text.	Weak language skills impede the meaning. The writing is error-ridden.

Argument Rubric

	10	5	1
Content	Includes strong topic/ issue and position (thesis) statements. Opposing claims/ rebuttals are presented logically and convincingly. Reasoning is backed with supporting statements.	Topic/issue and position (thesis) statements included but are vague. Opposing claims/ rebuttals are weak and do not present a clear, convincing argument. Supporting statements are not strong enough.	Lacking or weak topic/ issue and position (thesis) statements. Opposing claims/ rebuttals are not presented logically. Reasoning and supporting statements are not evident.
Organization and Structure	Introduction and conclusion are well written and effective. Follows one of the argument patterns. Progression of and transition between body paragraphs provides smooth, logical movement from one idea to the next. Unifying organization supports content.	Paper has introduction and conclusion, but the body isn't clearly organized with one of the argument patterns. Progression of and transition between body paragraphs is weak at some points. Content/ ideas would have been strengthened by a more unifying organization.	Lacking or poorly written introduction and/or conclusion. Paper doesn't follow one of the argument patterns. There is no logical progression of and transition between body paragraphs. Lacks a unifying organization, which made text difficult to follow.
Language	Correctly and accurately uses domain-specific and precise vocabulary. Includes compare-and-contrast sentences.	There is a limited use of domain-specific and precise vocabulary and compare-and-contrast sentences.	There is no use or inaccurate use of domain-specific vocabulary and compare-and-contrast sentences.
Grammar, Usage, Mechanics, and Spelling	Paper has only a few errors that do not distract or impede meaning.	There are several errors that potentially distract from the reading of the text.	Weak language skills impede the meaning. The writing is error-ridden.

Research Report Rubric

	10	5	1
Content	Information, facts, concrete details, quotations, or other examples are evident and relevant to the context of the paper. Extensive and applicable research is clear.	Information, facts, concrete details, quotations, or other examples are evident but not always relevant to the text. Better research would have strengthened the paper.	Lacks relevant information, facts, concrete details, quotations, or other examples. Little or no research is evident.
Organization and Structure	Introduction and conclusion are well written and effective. Organized to present a cohesive connection between ideas or information. There is a smooth, logical movement from one idea to the next. Overall unifying organization evident and effective.	Paper has introduction and conclusion, but the body isn't effectively organized. Progression of transition between ideas or information is weak at some points. Content/ideas would have been strengthened by a more unifying organization.	Lacking or poorly written introduction and/or conclusion. Paper doesn't present a cohesive connection between ideas or information. Lack of a unifying organization makes text difficult or impossible to follow.
Language	Correctly and accurately uses formal/academic language, domain-specific vocabulary, and precise wording.	Could improve use of formal/academic language, domain-specific vocabulary, and precise wording.	No use or inaccurate use of formal/academic language, domain-specific vocabulary, and precise wording.
Grammar, Usage, Mechanics, and Spelling	Paper has only a few errors that do not distract or impede meaning.	There are several errors that potentially distract from the reading of the text.	Weak language skills impede the meaning. The writing is error-ridden.

Document-Based Question Essay Rubric

	10	5	1
Content	• Comprehensively and clearly addresses the essay question. • Interprets documents correctly. • Includes a strong thesis. • Develops and provides sufficient supporting evidence. • Augments document data with relevant knowledge of social studies.	• Addresses most parts of the essay question. • Interprets some of the documents correctly • Includes a thesis statement • Develops and provides some supporting evidence • Rarely or weakly augments document's data with relevant knowledge of social studies	• Does not demonstrate understanding of the essay question. • Does not use and interpret documents correctly • Weak or nonexistent thesis statement and/or supporting evidence • Does not augment document's data with relevant knowledge of social studies
Text	• Includes strong introduction with historical context and makes reference to body paragraph's topics. • Body text cites, but does not copy, documents. • Includes topic sentences. • Has smooth and effective transitions between ideas. • Conclusion reiterates, but does not simply repeat, main idea and historical context.	• Includes introduction with some historical context and references to topics of the body paragraphs. • Body cites but seemingly copies documents. • Includes topic sentences. • Transitions between ideas are weak at some points. • Conclusion does not effectively reiterate main idea, thesis, and historical context	• Includes weak or nonexistent introduction (historical context and reference to body topics). • Does not include or includes very limited citations, topic sentences, and transitions between ideas.
Language	Correctly and accurately uses formal/academic language, domain-specific vocabulary, and precise wording.	Could improve use of formal/academic language, domain-specific vocabulary, and precise wording.	No use or inaccurate use of formal/academic language, domain-specific vocabulary, and precise wording.
Grammar, Usage, Mechanics, and Spelling	Paper has only a few errors that do not distract or impede meaning.	There are several errors that potentially distract from the reading of the text.	Weak language skills impede the meaning. The writing is error-ridden.

Recommended Literature

Bahti, Mark. 1988. *Pueblo Stories and Storytellers*. New York: Treasure Chest Publications.

Brandt, Keith, and Joann Early Macken. 2007. *Abraham Lincoln: Road to the White House*. New York: Scholastic.

Davidson, Margaret. 1991. *I Have a Dream: The Story of Martin Luther King*. New York: Scholastic Paperbacks.

Graff, Stewart, and Pollyanne Graff. 1999. *Helen Keller: Crusader for the Deaf and Blind*. New York: Yearling.

Hopkinson, Deborah. 2005. *John Adams Speaks for Freedom*. New York: Simon Spotlight.

Hrbek, Frank, and Andi Stix. 2013. *Active History: American Revolution*. Huntington Beach: Shell Education.

King, Stephen. 2001. *On Writing: A Memoir of the Craft*. New York: Simon & Schuster.

Kroll, Jennifer. 2010. *George Washington Carver: Planting Ideas*. Huntington Beach: Teacher Created Materials.

Krull, Kathleen. 1999. *Kid's Guide to America's Bill of Rights: Curfews, Censorship, and the 100-Pound Giant*. New York: Avon Books, Inc.

Lassieru, Allison. 2008. *The Attack on Pearl Harbor: An Interactive History Adventure*. North Mankato: Capstone Press.

McGovern, Ann. 1991. *If You Sailed on the Mayflower in 1620*. New York: Scholastic Paperbacks.

———. 1993. *The Pilgrims' First Thanksgiving*. New York: Scholastic Paperbacks.

Parks, Rosa, and Jim Haskins. 1999. *I Am Rosa Parks*. New York: Penguin Young Readers.

Stein, R. Conrad. 1986. *The Story of the Montgomery Bus Boycott*. New York: Children's Press.

Contents of the Digital Resources

The templates in this book are available as *Adobe*® PDFs online. Below is a complete list of the available documents. To access the digital resources, go to **www.tcmpub.com/download-files** and enter the following code: 88492245. Then, follow the on-screen directions. **Note:** Each of the PDF files listed includes a blank reproducible and a student exemplar (where applicable). Mentor text PDFs include annotated and unannotated copies.

Student Resources

Page Number	Title	Filename
26	Comparative Essay: Block Comparison	comparativeblock.pdf
35	Comparative Essay: Point-by-Point Comparison	comparativepoint.pdf
144	Thinking Through Your Writing	thinkingthrough.pdf
145	Add a Biographical Fact Planning Sheet	biofactplanning.pdf
146	Adding Facts Planning Sheet	addfactsplanning.pdf
147	Revising My Writing	revising.pdf
148	100 Critical Spelling Words	spellingwords.pdf
149	Troublesome Homophones	homophones.pdf
150	Partner Proofing	partnerproofing.pdf
151	AGO Teaching Plan	agoplan.pdf
152	Compare-and-Contrast Text Plan	comparecontrasttext.pdf
153	Sample Compare-and-Contrast Text	samplecomparecontrasttext.pdf
154	Compare-and-Contrast Sentences	comparecontrastsentences.pdf
155	Compare and Contrast: Search-and-Identify	searchidentify.pdf
156	Student Opinion Paper Guide	opinion.pdf
157	Topic, Issue, and Position Statement Planning Grid	planninggrid.pdf
158	How to Structure a Persuasive Essay	persuasiveessay.pdf
159	Opposing Reasons/Your Argument Planning Sheet	opposingargument.pdf
160	Argument T-Chart	argument.pdf
161	Explanatory Text Planning Web	explanatoryweb.pdf
162	Explanatory Text Planning Chart	explanatorychart.pdf
163	Pick a Great Combination of Transition Words	transitionwords.pdf
164	Thesis Web	thesisweb.pdf
165	Descriptive Writing	descriptive.pdf
166	Cause and Effect	causeeffect.pdf
167	Cause-and-Effect Sentences	causeeffectsentences.pdf
168	Cause-and-Effect Mapping	causeeffectmapping.pdf
169	Summary/Information Web	summaryweb.pdf
170	Writing Graph Summary Statements	graphsummary.pdf
171	Graph Sentences	graphsentences.pdf
172	Connection Sentences	connectionsentences.pdf
173	Vocabulary Pre-Test	vocabpretest.pdf

Contents of the Digital Resources (cont.)

174	Pre-Reading Vocabulary Assessment Sample	vocabassessmentsample.pdf
175	Pre-Reading Vocabulary Assessment	vocabassessment.pdf
176	Venn Diagram	venn.pdf
177	Triple Venn Diagram	triplevenn.pdf
178	Comparison Paragraph: How Subjects Are Alike	comparisonparagraph.pdf
179	Contrast Paragraph: How Subjects Are Not Alike	contrastparagraph.pdf
180	Nouns, Verbs, and Adjectives	nounsverbsadjectives.pdf
181	Nouns, Verbs, and Adjectives Text	nounsverbsadjectivestext.pdf
182	Word Mastery	wordmastery.pdf
183	Two-Voice Poems	twovoice.pdf
184	Two-Voice Poems: Senate and House of Representatives	twovoiceSenateHouse.pdf
185	Lunes	lunes.pdf
186	Cinquains	cinquains.pdf
187	Acrostics	acrostics.pdf
188	"I Believe" Poems	believe.pdf
189	"I Am from" Poems	iamfrom.pdf

Mobiles/Graphics

Page Number	Title	Filename
190	The Editing Process	editing.pdf
191	Introduction, Body, Conclusion	introbodyconclusion.pdf
192	Paragraph Mobile	paragraph.pdf
193	Five Paragraph Essay	fiveparagraph.pdf

Rubrics

Page Number	Title	Filename
194	Compare-and-Contrast Rubric	comparecontrastrubric.pdf
195	Argument Rubric	argumentrubric.pdf
196	Research Report Rubric	researchrubric.pdf
197	Document-Based Question Essay Rubric	DBQrubric.pdf

Mentor Texts

Page Numbers	Title	Filename
120–121	Two Houses of Congress Block Comparisons	mentortext1.pdf
122–123	Two Houses of Congress Point-by-Point	mentortext2.pdf
124–125	Battle of the Alamo	mentortext3.pdf
126–127	House Rules	mentortext4.pdf
128–129	School Uniforms Point-by-Point	mentortext5.pdf
130–131	School Uniforms Opposition/Rebuttal	mentortext6.pdf
132	Research Report: New Deal	mentortext7.pdf